SOCIAL EMOTIONAL LEARNING

AND THE BRAIN

ASCD MEMBER BOOK

Many ASCD members received this book
as a member benefit upon its initial release.

Learn more at **www.ascd.org/memberbooks**

ALSO BY THE AUTHOR

101 Strategies to Make Academic Vocabulary Stick

Brain-Based Teaching in the Digital Age

Everyday Vocabulary Strategies (Quick Reference Guide)

How to Teach So Students Remember, 2nd Edition

*Teaching the Critical Vocabulary of the Common Core:
55 Words That Make or Break Student Understanding*

*Vocab Rehab: How do I teach vocabulary effectively
with limited time? (ASCD Arias)*

SOCIAL EMOTIONAL LEARNING AND THE BRAIN

Strategies
to Help Your
Students Thrive

— MARILEE
SPRENGER —

ASCD

Alexandria, Virginia USA

1703 N. Beauregard St. • Alexandria, VA 22311-1714 USA
Phone: 800-933-2723 or 703-578-9600 • Fax: 703-575-5400
Website: www.ascd.org • E-mail: member@ascd.org
Author guidelines: www.ascd.org/write

Ranjit Sidhu, *CEO & Executive Director;* Stefani Roth, *Publisher;* Genny Ostertag, *Director, Content Acquisitions;* Allison Scott, *Acquisitions Editor;* Julie Houtz, *Director, Book Editing & Production;* Miriam Calderone, *Editor;* Judi Connelly, *Senior Art Director;* Masie Chong, *Graphic Designer;* Valerie Younkin, *Senior Production Designer;* Kelly Marshall, *Manager, Production Services;* Trinay Blake, *E-Publishing Specialist*

All web links in this book are correct as of the publication date below but may have become inactive or otherwise modified since that time. If you notice a deactivated or changed link, please e-mail books@ascd.org with the words "Link Update" in the subject line. In your message, please specify the web link, the book title, and the page number on which the link appears.

PAPERBACK ISBN: 978-1-4166-2949-8   ASCD product #121010

PDF E-BOOK ISBN: 978-1-4166-2951-1; see Books in Print for other formats.

Quantity discounts are available: e-mail programteam@ascd.org or call 800-933-2723, ext. 5773, or 703-575-5773. For desk copies, go to www.ascd.org/deskcopy.

ASCD Member Book No. FY21-1 (Sep 2020 PSI+). ASCD Member Books mail to Premium (P), Select (S), and Institutional Plus (I+) members on this schedule: Jan, PSI+; Feb, P; Apr, PSI+; May, P; Jul, PSI+; Aug, P; Sep, PSI+; Nov, PSI+; Dec, P. For current details on membership, see www.ascd.org/membership.

Library of Congress Cataloging-in-Publication Data
Library of Congress Cataloging-in-Publication Data
Names: Sprenger, Marilee, 1949- author.
Title: Social-emotional learning and the brain : strategies to help your students thrive / Marilee Sprenger.
Description: Alexandria, VA : ASCD, 2020. | Includes bibliographical references and index.
Identifiers: LCCN 2020022066 (print) | LCCN 2020022067 (ebook) | ISBN 9781416629498 (paperback) | ISBN 9781416629511 (pdf)
Subjects: LCSH: Affective education. | Cognitive neuroscience. | Teacher-student relationships—Psychological aspects. | Brain.
Classification: LCC LB1072 .S68 2020 (print) | LCC LB1072 (ebook) | DDC 370.15/34—dc23
LC record available at https://lccn.loc.gov/2020022066
LC ebook record available at https://lccn.loc.gov/2020022067

29 28 27 26 25 24 23 22 21 20   1 2 3 4 5 6 7 8 9 10 11 12

*I dedicate this book to all the
students who needed an adult in their life to help
them cope, overcome, and succeed. We didn't
know better. We are trying to do better.*

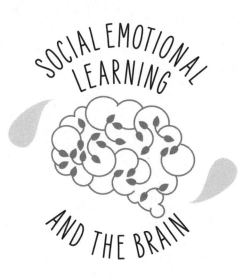

SOCIAL EMOTIONAL LEARNING AND THE BRAIN

Acknowledgments

There are many to thank for helping this book come to fruition. Stefani Roth, Genny Ostertag, and Allison Scott saw the need for a book connecting brain research to social-emotional learning. Without their support, this would not have come at such an important time for all students and educators. I wish to also thank Miriam Calderone, who always makes me sound so much better. She is an extraordinary editor, and I so appreciate her help.

The experts in the field are many, so I will try to mention those whose work affected me most. Dr. Nadine-Burke Harris, Dr. Bessel van der Kolk, Dr. Dan Siegel, Dr. David Sousa, Dr. Eric Jensen, Dr. Pat Wolfe, Dr. Judy Willis, Dr. Mary Helen Immordino-Yang, Dr. Bob Sapolsky, Dr. Bruce Perry, and Dr. Lori Desautels all added to my knowledge about the brain and the effects of emotions, stress, and trauma on the brain and body.

To Doug Fisher, Nancy Frey, Maurice Elias, Michele Borba, Marc Brackett, Matt Liebowitz, Lisa Barrett, Michael McKnight, Thomas Armstrong, Meena Srinivasan, and Mr. Fred Rogers: thank you all for your contributions to this field to help our students succeed in school and in life.

Always, I am grateful for the love and support of my husband, Scott.

Introduction

Two things should become foundational in our education system: social-emotional learning (SEL) and trauma-informed practices. As educators, we know that many of our students have been affected by adverse childhood experiences (ACEs) and that positive childhood experiences can counteract some of the resulting trauma. Social-emotional learning has the power to create some of those positive experiences. Furthermore, many of the SEL strategies overlap with those related to trauma-informed practices.

A recurring theme in this book is that every child has a story, and I hope that the information shared in the following pages will help rewrite some of those stories and reinforce others. The path for educators is clear: build relationships so students feel love and a sense of belonging; teach empathy so students feel understood and can provide understanding to others; make students self-aware so that feelings are understood; help students regulate feelings so they can attain and use prosocial skills; support students in becoming skilled in social awareness so they build an understanding of how to interact with people; teach students how to handle relationships so they can work and play with people who come from various backgrounds and cultures; and finally, teach students how to choose and make wise decisions that will affect the future.

It bears repeating: every child has a story. I have a story. I am one of those adults who grew up believing that I was not good enough, that I could not fit in (although I pretended to), let alone belong anywhere. I grew up with rules that no child should grow up with: don't show your feelings; never, ever cry or your mom will leave you; never trust others—especially men (they will cheat and leave). I am one of every six adults who has experienced four or more ACEs during my lifetime (Centers for Disease Control and Prevention, n.d.). I know the fight-or-flight response well. As a result, my physical and mental health are at risk.

I am not sharing this information to elicit pity. Many people have had far worse experiences than mine. I did not live in poverty; I had two parents at home; I had the food, clothing, and shelter that I needed. I am sharing this information because of the two people who saved me, who literally kept me from the depression and despair hovering over me as a child, who made me realize that even though I never knew what would happen at home, I could go to the dependable, positive place that was school. Those two people were teachers. My 1st grade teacher, Miss Pauli, let me come in early to her beautiful, welcoming classroom, and she let me talk. She listened. She complimented my work and encouraged me. Fast-forward to 5th grade. Miss Williams made me feel important, that I was good enough. She is the reason, beyond any doubt, why I became a teacher. I wanted to make kids feel the way she had made me feel. She listened, she cared, she touched—gentle hugs and pats on the head or shoulder—and she checked in throughout the day to make sure we were all OK. A few other people were positive influences along the way, and I was OK until my first depressive episode in college. I eventually sought the help I needed, and I am doing well.

But I'm worried about the kids. According to John Medina (2017), humans today could live to be 115 to 122, under ideal conditions. Perhaps those conditions include healthy eating and getting enough exercise, but they must certainly also include lower levels of stress, positive relationships, family ties (within the family you were born into or the family you create), feeling empathy for and from others, and having a sense of belonging. Social-emotional learning addresses all those conditions. Furthermore, SEL improves academic achievement by an average of 11 percent, increases appropriate social behavior, improves students' attitudes, and reduces depression and stress (Durlak, Weissberg, Dymnicki, Taylor, & Schellinger, 2011).

I have been a student of the brain since 1992. I have traveled, trained, and spoken with educational leader and author Eric Jensen, who has taught me much about the brain and how to find out more. Through my research, I have identified the connections in the brain that are related to the social-emotional learning competencies delineated by the Collaborative for Academic, Social, and Emotional Learning (CASEL): self-awareness, self-management, social awareness, relationship skills, and responsible decision making. This organization, which began as a group of educators and researchers committed to advancing social-emotional learning, has had a huge impact in this area for more than 20 years.

By following the work of Daniel Goleman, one of the cofounders of CASEL and author of the groundbreaking book *Emotional Intelligence* (1995), and the work of neuroscientists such as Bessel van der Kolk (2014), we can see how SEL affects various areas of the brain. For instance, in this book you will learn how our "gut feelings" are directly related to the decision-making areas in our brain.

In reading the work of Daniel Kahneman, author of the best-selling book *Thinking, Fast and Slow* (2011), we learn about the brain's two thinking systems. System 1 is fast, automatic, emotional, and unconscious. System 2 is slow, effortful, and conscious. System 1 is at work when our students react *without* thinking. SEL strategies will teach students to stop and use System 2 before they respond. One of the strategies I used with my students when they needed to respond in a situation was to ask this question: "Are you checking System 2, or is System 1 in charge?" The more students practice taking a breath and giving some thought to a situation or decision, the more likely they are to respond appropriately.

From brain structures to brain chemicals, learning takes place on an emotional level. Awareness of emotions and being able to regulate those emotions lead the way to building positive relationships, successfully solving problems, and making responsible decisions. Understanding the brain helps both students and teachers rely on strategies that will activate the appropriate parts of the brain and will be suitable for whatever experience they encounter. For example, when students know that getting upset activates the *limbic* (emotional) brain and blocks the connection between the thinking brain and the emotional brain, they realize the importance of having and using strategies to calm themselves before speaking or acting.

Brain Structures and Chemicals Related to SEL

One of the simpler ways to look at the brain is from the bottom to the top. The spinal cord is connected to the *brain stem,* the lowermost part of the brain. The brain stem contains the first filtering system for information that comes into the brain via our senses. This system is called the *reticular activating system,* or RAS; it filters out about 99 percent of incoming information. If the information entering is in some way threatening, the RAS may halt the flow of information in favor of sending out an alarm throughout the brain. When the next level, the *limbic system,* receives the alarm, many activities begin. First, the *amygdala,* the brain's second filter, examines the information. The *hypothalamus,* which is part of the limbic system, sends out chemicals to prepare the body and brain for a fight-or-flight response. Other chemicals, such as *adrenaline,* which is released from the adrenal glands, cause the heart to beat faster and increase the rate of breathing. Unless the body is in immediate danger, whatever the stressor is, the thinking brain should decide what next steps to take. But the pathway from the thinking brain (the *frontal lobe;* in particular, the *prefrontal cortex*) down to the reflexive brain (the limbic system and the brain stem) is slow. If we put all our focus on the amygdala, the limbic structure in charge of emotions, it will (along with the *hippocampus,* a structure related to memory) bring to mind all the horrors of this particular stress-inducing phenomenon. For example, if we are approaching a large German shepherd and previously had a bad experience with a similar dog, that memory will drive our brain and we will expect a repetition of the bad incident.

Emotions influence where new information is processed in the brain. For learning to become memory, it must be directed through the emotional filter (the amygdala) along the route to the reflective, higher brain—the prefrontal cortex. When this happens, the brain takes a responsible look at the situation and finds a better way to handle it. Perhaps, in the German shepherd example, the thinking brain will notice that this dog is on a leash and would be unable to reach us.

Several chemical "cocktails" run our brains. *Neurotransmitters* such as dopamine, serotonin, endorphins, and oxytocin are some of the most common. Cortisol, the stress hormone, is also involved in many situations, both positive and negative. Cortisol is released when we are a little anxious about a presentation, an interview, or meeting someone for the first time—examples of good stress. It is also released when our brains are preparing for survival. That fight, flight, or freeze situation—bad stress—prompts the release of much more cortisol.

And what is the antidote to stress? According to Foreman (2019), the antidote is trust.

I have created the word *selebrate* to define the premise of my work. *Selebrate* stands for "social-emotional learning elicits brain responses appropriate to experience." It's a lot to say, but it says a lot. Social-emotional learning should help our students choose the appropriate response in whatever situation they may find themselves. Neuroscience researchers have found areas and chemicals in the brain that respond to certain learning strategies. I want us to be able to understand why a response occurs and then create more strategies that will engage the same areas of the brain.

Don't Let Emotion Drive the Bus!

Mo Willems's book *Don't Let the Pigeon Drive the Bus!* was a favorite of my youngest granddaughter, Maeve, so I read it to her often. I also used it as the inspiration for her birthday book, which is a collection of photos from throughout the year that I usually make into some kind of story (I do one every year for each of my grandchildren). Maeve's fifth book, titled *Don't Let Maeve Drive the Bus!*, was filled with wonderful things that Maeve could do, like playing soccer, reading, and climbing, but it conveyed the message that we would never want a 5-year-old to drive!

Along those same lines, we don't want emotions driving our lives. Adding to our lives? Yes. Driving our learning? Yes. My friend Robert Sylwester, author of *A Celebration of Neurons* (1995), tells us that "emotions drive attention, which drives learning, memory, and just about everything else" (p. 99). But we should also keep in mind Brené Brown's warning against emotion as the sole driver of learning: "If emotion is driving, where is logic and thought? In the back seat? Or worse, in the trunk!" (Jarvis, 2019).

Storytelling in the Brain

The power of storytelling can be traced to the brain and its chemical reactions. Whether reading a story or listening to one, it appears that a specific cascade of chemicals is involved in the engagement. Think of yourself listening to a story. Because it is about something unknown, your brain releases the stress hormone cortisol. This release occurs not because of fear or anger but, rather, curiosity. You are ready for the novelty and perhaps suspense. Dopamine is also released to keep you focused on what is going to happen. Because this is a novel situation (an unknown story), you must be prepared for anything and remain on task until you know the ending. Novelty engages the brain because something novel may also be dangerous. Survival first! Dopamine rewards us by keeping us alert and getting to the goal—the end of the story. When we identify with characters in the story, oxytocin is released. Oxytocin is the trust chemical, the "friending juice" in the brain. It has often been described as the "love" or "cuddle" chemical. According to Paul Zak (2013), director of the Center for Neuroeconomics Studies and professor of economics, psychology, and management at Claremont Graduate University, experiments show that character-driven stories with emotional content result in a better understanding of key points and better recall of the information.

One of the primary questions I have sought to answer in this book is this: because storytelling is so powerful and memorable, what other strategies will cause the release of the same chemicals to provide lasting memories and good feelings? One answer that is addressed in this book is role-playing.

Chapter Overview

As I discovered which brain structures and chemicals were involved in the SEL competencies mentioned previously, the next step was to find strategies that would activate the brain in the same way. Explanations of those strategies make up much of the content of this book. However, in addition to incorporating SEL strategies into their instruction, teachers need to examine the SEL competencies for themselves. As I worked on each chapter, I asked myself questions such as these: *How self-aware am I? Can I name and tame my emotions? Do I make sure I am aware of my students' perspectives? How can I teach students to handle relationships with others if I may be having relationship issues myself? Do I make responsible decisions when I am interacting at school?* Here is an overview of the chapters that follow.

Chapter 1: Building Teacher-Student Relationships

The teacher-student relationship is the primary component of and precursor to a true social-emotional learning environment. In this chapter, I discuss building relationships with students and share various strategies. The mantra of many teachers who are interested in SEL and want to begin to implement trauma-informed practices is "Maslow before Bloom," a concept whose essence is the idea that dealing with students' needs first will allow us to remove some possible barriers to learning.

Chapter 2: Empathy

According to experts, empathy is a major problem for today's students (Borba, 2016). In this chapter, I define different types of empathy and describe how, throughout brain development, we can see where activity related to empathy is located and which chemicals are released during empathic episodes. Some neuroscientists believe that empathy leads us to compassion, and these two ideas are considered. I share examples of what empathic students do and how empathy can be modeled, as well as strategies to teach empathy and compassion to all students.

Chapter 3: Self-Awareness

In this chapter, I define and discuss the first SEL competency as delineated by CASEL: self-awareness. Recognizing our own emotions is vital to the SEL process; identifying emotions in ourselves allows us to recognize those emotions in others. In addition, teaching students to recognize and name their own emotions leads them to the ability to manage those emotions. Which emotions are innate and which are learned is also a focus of this chapter. Finally, I present strategies for teaching and modeling self-awareness.

Chapter 4: Self-Management

One of teachers' greatest concerns is dealing with behavior issues. Research supports the belief that students' ability to manage their own emotions is key to changing some undesirable behaviors. In this chapter, I identify areas of the brain related to self-management and discuss the struggles between brain structures. I also address stress and ways to manage it, as well as the importance of classroom rituals and routines pertaining to managing and eliciting brain states with stories and examples. Strategies for teaching self-management skills, from the "CBS method" to the "break-up letter," cover all grade levels.

Chapter 5: Social Awareness

From self-management we move into social awareness—helping students become more sensitive to the feelings of others. In this chapter, I explain that once students can recognize and manage their own emotions, they are ready to interact with others in an emotionally intelligent way. An examination of areas in the brain related to social awareness leads to a discussion of social pain and the ways that bullying can affect others. As students gain empathy skills, we can teach and practice social awareness strategies.

Chapter 6: Relationship Skills

The focus in Chapter 1 was on building our relationships with our students. In this chapter, the focus is on teaching students how to handle their own relationships. Beginning with finding which areas of the brain are active when handling relationships in an empathic way and then focusing on brain states and peer pressure, the discussion concludes with strategies that we can use every day to build this important SEL competency.

Chapter 7: Responsible Decision Making

As the prefrontal cortex continues to grow and develop, making responsible decisions should become easier for students. That development is dependent on how often they are offered the opportunity to make decisions. This chapter focuses on helping students identify their values and beliefs for decision making. With the other competencies addressed, students will be able to understand how their decisions affect others in the present and the future. Teaching students how to be a role model for others in this arena includes modeling our own decision-making process, offering choices and discussing possible outcomes, and providing group work to further the applications and results of good decision making.

Chapter 8: People, Not Programs: The Positive Impact of SEL

According to Bruce Perry, child psychiatrist and senior fellow of the Child Trauma Academy in Houston, Texas, programs don't change people—*people* change people! With this in mind, this chapter addresses how to promote the use of SEL every day for teachers and for students. It also emphasizes the need for positive childhood experiences to counterbalance adverse childhood experiences. All students can benefit from schools that implement SEL and trauma-informed practices. At a minimum, schools using

SEL need to be aware of and sensitive to the effects of trauma. This chapter also provides resources for digging deeper into these topics.

1

Building Teacher-Student Relationships

The brain is most interested in survival and has a deep need for relating to others.

—John Medina

If you read no other chapter in this book, read this one. This reading alone will make a big impact in your classroom—as it could in *every* classroom. Building and maintaining relationships is the core of life. The central role of relationships is also backed by research. According to Hattie (2017), positive relationships between teacher and student have an effect size on learning of 0.52. The effect size is a measure of how important a difference is between two groups. This means that based on a meta-analysis of relationships, teacher-student relationships can accelerate learning more than the average 0.40, which represents a year's worth of growth. Before we can teach students how to handle relationships with their peers, we, as educators, need to model relationship building.

14   Social-Emotional Learning and the Brain

When it comes to the subject of history, there isn't a finer teacher than Sarah. She loves her content and can often mesmerize her students with stories, monologues, and rare tidbits of information about a country's war heroes and relationships, both personal and professional. When the school survey was given to 6th through 12th grade students, however, Sarah did not fare well.

She was crushed when she reviewed the answers her students gave in several areas. Although 88 percent of her students agreed that Sarah explained things in a different way if students didn't understand, only 15 percent said that she noticed when they were having difficulty, and only 5 percent said that she helped them when they were upset.

At first, Sarah was angry. She thought, "With all the time I spend preparing the best lessons for them, making sure that I help them see and hear history, how can they say I don't notice their content and personal issues? What's wrong with them?"

By the time Mr. Mercer called her in for a meeting to discuss the results, Sarah had begun to calm down and was trying to figure out how the students had come to their conclusions. She sat down across from her principal and mentor. He smiled and began by saying, "Sarah, you know you are a great teacher and you reach most of your students. Your teaching style is above reproach. My observations in your classroom have shown me how you can dazzle reluctant learners, and whether I'm observing your 8th graders absorbing the nuances of the Civil War or your 10th graders tackling the reasons leading up to the war in Vietnam, your kids view you as a knowledgeable historian. You can make them feel connected to Holocaust victims and survivors, but you don't seem to make them feel connected to you! It wasn't until I studied the surveys that I realized this.

"I apologize for not looking closely enough to realize that you have a relationship with your class, but you don't really relate to your individual students. That is, you don't have a personal relationship with them. Your dynamic presentation of material draws them to the content, but you must establish a way to draw them to you. They need to trust you as a person. Many of them need to feel noticed as individuals. Seventy-four percent say that you give them specific suggestions for improving their work, and out of the 150 students you teach, that says a lot. But only 25 percent say that you support them both inside and outside the classroom. Let's talk about what you can do to increase this. You see, the students who are upset about this are the ones who can't get your full attention, the kids who need to know someone cares about them, not just their content or their grades.

"It's not always easy to build relationships with pre-adolescents and adolescents. You and the other adults in their lives are their last best chance to get beyond some of the trauma and stress they experience—many on a daily basis."

At this, Sarah sat back in her chair and sighed. "Mr. Mercer, I've never been good with relationships. Even though I can conjure up unusual and interesting lessons, I don't relate to people well. I think I need to take a course!"

Sarah isn't the only one with this problem. If you ask adults how many teachers they had meaningful relationships with—that is, how many teachers they trusted and knew cared about them—most respondents would probably come up with only one or two from grades K–12 and most likely none at the university level.

But the brain isn't finished developing until the mid-20s, and it needs so much guidance! When we ignore the importance of meaningful teacher-student relationships, we miss opportunities to help our students grow and relate to others in their world. Whether you teach kindergartners or postgraduate students, building relationships with those brains that are entrusted to you—even for just a few hours per week—offers the largest payoff in terms of learning and working in a world full of people with whom relationships can be life-changing. In other words, *relationships should come first* in the classroom, the staff room, and the board room. The goal should be to prepare our students for making lasting connections throughout their lives.

Maslow Before Bloom

"You can't take care of the Bloom stuff until you take care of the Maslow stuff!" says Alan Beck (1994), founder of Advantage Academy. Beck was born into poverty, but with the help of various teachers along the way, he became a successful student, attained a PhD, and pursued a successful career in education that eventually led to opening the academy. He pledged to teach students in a way that provides hope for the future.

Beck's comment about Bloom and Maslow refers to the work of Benjamin Bloom (Bloom, Engelhart, Furst, Hill, & Krathwohl, 1956) and Abraham Maslow (1998). Most teachers have a basic knowledge of the work of Abraham Maslow, who created a hierarchy of human needs. They also are aware of the push to use Bloom's taxonomy, a hierarchy of learning objectives classified into levels of complexity. Bloom's work is usually presented only in the cognitive domain, leaving out the affective and sensory domains. However, getting our students up the scale of Bloom's taxonomy is impossible without first meeting their basic needs. Too often our traditional approach to education has focused on levels of cognitive learning, leading up to higher-order thinking and largely ignoring students' needs.

Today, many schools and organizations are focusing on Maslow's hierarchy. But in my most recent book on memory, *How to Teach So Students Remember* (Sprenger, 2018), I offer a comparison between Maslow's hierarchy and the hierarchy presented by

Matthew Lieberman (2013), who believes that Maslow had it wrong. Maslow's hierarchy arranges basic needs this way: physiological, safety, belonging and love, esteem, and self-actualization. Lieberman, in contrast, believes that we should begin with belonging and love. He argues that it is relationships that provide us with our physiological needs and safety needs. Think of an infant who needs food or a diaper change or warmth. The infant obtains those things through crying to get the attention of a caregiver. Following Lieberman's view, I like to present the argument that our students hold their social needs above some of their physiological needs. (Think of the 7th grade girl who almost wets her pants rather than run to the restroom because teams are being chosen for volleyball.) Belonging comes first! (I describe Lieberman's research on social pain, a related concept, in Chapter 5.)

Getting back to the quote from Alan Beck, social-emotional learning gives students the opportunity to deal with stress and anxiety, so they will be able to focus on higher-level thinking. Maslow before Bloom!

Relationships in the Brain

When studying the brain, neuroscientists look at both structures and chemical reactions. The *frontal lobe* houses the structures where most brain activity occurs when people care about each other, trust each other, and want to be friends. The *limbic system* houses the *amygdala,* the seat of emotion. The limbic system is loaded with receptors for chemicals for two different hormonal systems: the stress-response system and the trust/love system (Cantor, 2019). (See Figure 1.1.) When we are stressed, *cortisol* is released, triggering the stress response. By contrast, when we care about and trust someone, *oxytocin* is released and we feel connected.

Figure 1.1
Relationships in the Brain

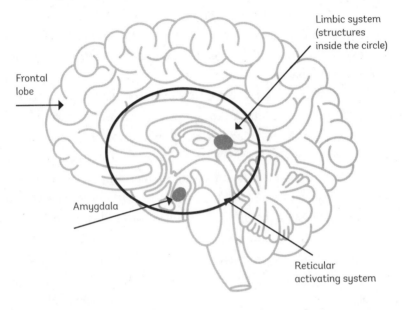

A true connection goes deeper than casual acquaintance. Rather, it involves someone who offers motivation, excitement, or even comfort. When we begin a relationship, the brain releases *dopamine, noradrenaline,* and, as just mentioned, *oxytocin* (Pearce, Wlodarski, Machin, & Dunbar, 2017). The limbic system is stimulated and the reticular activating system (the brain's first filter) in the brain stem is relaxed, which allows new information to enter the brain in a calm way and make its way up to the limbic system. Dopamine is the brain's "seeking" chemical (Davis & Montag, 2019); it keeps us working toward a goal and stimulates our brain's reward system. When we connect with others, we feel good about ourselves and the other person. Noradrenaline is an excitatory chemical. Oxytocin, as noted, is released when we feel an attachment. Once a relationship is established with someone, even thinking about that person can cause the release of oxytocin and dopamine.

Strategies for Building Teacher-Student Relationships

As I mentioned in the introduction to this book, I created the word *selebrate* to stand for "social-emotional learning elicits brain responses appropriate to experience." Many researchers (including Nadine Burke Harris, Bruce Perry, Marc Hackett, Eric Jensen, and David Sousa) tell us that a single relationship with an adult can change the course of a student's life. Classroom teachers probably spend more time with students than any other adults. This is an opportunity to model appropriate social interactions, show students that we care for them, and support them in their endeavors. These may sound like parental responsibilities, but our children—our future citizens—are everyone's responsibility. We can positively affect our students' brains. Educational consultant and author Horatio Sanchez (2015) says, "For the brain to do anything, chemical movements have to occur. Health is the ability to manage all the different chemicals the brain produces within a normative range at all times." This ability creates a kind of *homeostasis*—a state of internal balance and stability among interdependent elements. The following strategies are intended to help teachers help their students reach this level of balance and stability.

Display Vulnerability

Researcher, author, and public speaker Brené Brown (2018) has addressed the need for displaying vulnerability in our lives and in our relationships. We need to model for students that we are willing to be vulnerable (which includes being honest and transparent) and create a safe space for them to do so, too. Displaying vulnerability ranges from admitting you are feeling tired and irritated after an all-nighter with a sick child to acknowledging that you grabbed the wrong assessment from your file and, as a result, students were asked some questions that had not been discussed in class. For students, it can range from attempting to answer a question when they are not sure they are correct to admitting they overreacted to a remark from another student. When our students show up, put forth effort, and fail, it's important to let them know that we all have those experiences and it's OK. We understand one another, and we keep going.

One of my favorite Brené Brown suggestions is to say, "This is the story I am telling myself right now . . ." and then explain how you are feeling about what is happening. For instance, "The story I am telling myself right now is that you are upset with me or someone in the class, and that is driving the behavior I am seeing. Is my story correct?" From this point, you can usually lead students to tell their story.

Greet Students at the Door

A recent study suggests that greeting and welcoming students each morning increased achievement by 20 percent and lowered disruptive behaviors by 9 percent (Cook, Fiat, & Larson, 2018). The study included the following suggestions for teachers:

- Say the student's name.
- Make eye contact.
- Use a friendly nonverbal greeting, such as a handshake, high five, or thumbs-up.
- Give a few words of encouragement.
- Ask students how their day is going.

My granddaughter once said to me, "My favorite part of coming to your house is knowing you'll be waiting at the door to see us! How do you know exactly when we will be there?" In response, I said, "It's simple, Maeve. When you look forward to seeing someone—you know, that 'I can't wait' feeling—you make that foremost in your mind. I ask your parents to text me when you are close, and I wait at the door. I always greet my students at the door to let them know how excited I am to see them and that I care about them!"

And so I did—and I do. The truth? As a teacher, I couldn't wait to see most students, but I had to be there for *all* of them; so I was always at the door to greet them. In fact, some classes waited outside the door until I showed up to welcome them in. I did this every day, for every class. And it made a difference. For those who did not appear to be receptive, I was still there, smiling, saying, "Good morning" or "Hello" or just "Happy to see you!"

They were 5th graders. It was a tough school, a tough crowd. It was hard for me to believe that 11-year-olds could be scary— that is, until I stood before them. I was acting assistant principal when one of our 5th grade teachers divorced her husband, broke her contract, and moved away with her two kids. She had been struggling for months with her marriage and had used up all her sick days for mental health reasons and to see her attorney.

The students at this school came from backgrounds of generational poverty or broken homes or had a parent in prison. They had trusted this teacher, and slowly, over time, she had let them down, just as their parents had let them down. When she left, the students trusted no one and found yet again that they were alone in the world. They were angry. And we know that anger is the bodyguard of fear. They were afraid to trust. After several subs came and went, we decided that I would take over this class until the end of the year.

We were one month into the second semester. I stood at the door that first morning to shake their hands and say hello. Only 2 of the 24 students reciprocated with a handshake. Most looked at me blankly. One of the students, Jamail, said, "What are you doing here? Who's in trouble?"

After they all entered and were seated, I turned off the music I had playing. I explained that I was going to be their teacher and hoped that we could all work together to make the class and learning successful for everyone.

Every day I stood at the door to greet them and shake their hands. Every day the response was the same. I thought about giving up on the morning greeting. The students had felt abandoned; I was feeling rejected.

In time, the students responded somewhat to the brain-compatible learning strategies that I used. They began to feel more successful as they interacted with one another, worked in cooperative groups, and became more aware of others' feelings as well as their own. It was the social-emotional learning connection that made a difference.

After 17 mornings of my standing by the door to greet them, the "leader of the pack" reached out to shake my hand. Quinn, the best-dressed and cockiest student of all, shook my hand and echoed back my greeting when he said, "Good morning. I'm glad you're here today." Was he just mocking me? It didn't matter. At least it was a response!

After that, the other students slowly followed suit. What made the difference? It wasn't my persistence. It wasn't my smile. They didn't feel sorry for me because no one would respond. It was the fact that I was there—every day. I showed up. I couldn't dare be absent. They had to see that they could again count on someone.

No one has to explain to you how to greet a friend, but, after making eye contact and saying the person's name, you can make a greeting more powerful by doing one of the following:

- **Ask a question:** What's your favorite _____? (You can ask about color, season, food, kind of pizza, animal, and so on.)
- **Make a request:** I could use your help with a bulletin board. (Alternatives might include using an app, solving a problem, or taking attendance.)

- **Use nonverbal signals:** These may include smiles, high fives, handshakes, hugs. (It took a long time before some students would let me touch them—particularly those who had been mistreated or abused in some way. Be patient and know that some students may never let you touch them.)

You Say Hello; You Say Goodbye

Welcoming students with a greeting is a great strategy, but saying goodbye can be just as important. Teachers in middle and high school may have difficulty with this, but leaving your last-period classroom and being in the hall when students are packing up at their lockers and heading out the door can be powerful. They will know that you care when you leave your desk and papers for a few minutes to say goodbye, remind them about an assignment, or tell them you look forward to seeing them tomorrow. That tough group of 5th graders softened up even more at the end of the day. Helping pack up a backpack, asking how their day was, and just saying, "See you tomorrow!" let them know I cared and would be there for them. It was a little sad yet heartwarming when a few of the kids leaving would ask, "See you tomorrow?"

Tell Your Story

One strategy that has been heavily researched is storytelling. As Burton (2019) tells us, our brain takes information and puts it in story form as it tries to make sense of the world. Research has uncovered the "chemical cocktail" that occurs in the brain when we listen to or read a story. First, dopamine is released as we derive pleasure from listening to the story. Small amounts of cortisol are released when there is some distress or uncertainty as "the plot thickens." Finally, oxytocin is released as we relate to the characters and learn the outcome. Dopamine is released again as a reward—that is, the satisfaction and pleasure derived from the solution to the problem or the outcome of the story.

What does storytelling have to do with relationships? Everything. It begins with your relationships with your students. Talking about yourself, your family, and your activities helps build rapport with your students. Involving them in a problem and asking them to help provides a solution that connects them to you.

For instance, in one large 6th grade class consisting of 32 students (21 boys and 11 girls), it wasn't easy to get to know each student quickly. Their teacher, Mrs. Tate, often began each day with a story relating to the content (history or literature) that would be covered that day, and she would try to put the students in the story. When they studied the Civil War, she might begin a story like this: "Imagine yourself wanting to join your friends to save your 'country.' You are out to protect your family, your home, and possibly your freedom. You put on a heavy uniform, if you have one. In the early days of the war, not everyone had a uniform. To make matters more complicated, you might have a blue uniform. This was tricky. If you were fighting for the South, the Confederacy, you were to wear gray. The Northerners, the Union, were the ones who wore blue. So if you fought for the South and all you had to wear was a blue uniform, you could get shot by your own side! What would you do to keep yourself safe?"

A story like this focuses students on the content and their own emotions—and strengthens their relationship with Mrs. Tate. In essence, she is asking each individual student in the class what they would do. The question elevates them to a sense that "we're all in this together."

Use Five Ways to Show You Care

It was Teddy Roosevelt who said, "Nobody cares how much you know until they know how much you care." Letting students know that you truly do care about them is often easier with younger kids than with preteens and teenagers. Students need to know we care, and here are five ways, according to Fisher and Frey (2019), to show we are invested in relationships with them:

- **Providing structure:** Rules should be fair and apply to all; having consistent expectations for every student is key.
- **Offering choice:** Students, particularly teens, seek autonomy, and when possible, they need to be involved in decisions that are going to affect them personally.
- **Showing interest:** Discovering information about their lives, asking questions about their music, and attending their athletic events (or at least knowing the scores) are ways to demonstrate your interest.
- **Being optimistic:** Express to students through speech and actions that you believe in their ability to succeed.
- **Acknowledging their feelings:** Show emotional support and help them process their feelings.

Keeping these things in mind, let's consider middle to high school students. Their schedules don't allow for a lot of one-on-one time. In addition, teachers who have five or six different classes each day have less time to build relationships. Nevertheless, making the effort to do so is well worth it.

Write Notes to Students

Keep envelopes with each student's name in your desk and occasionally write notes to students. Let students know what you appreciate about them or how you liked some of their work. You might keep the envelopes in a file, and after you give a student a letter, put that student's envelope at the back of the bunch. This way you can be certain to reach out to every student.

Stick It to Them

In a variation of the note-writing strategy, keep a stack of sticky notes handy, and whenever a student does something that you want to point out, write it on a sticky note and put the note on the student's desk, locker, or notebook. The note can be anything from

"You played a great game last night!" to "I saw you helping the new student, and I'm sure he appreciated it!"

Be a Name-Caller

Self-improvement author and lecturer Dale Carnegie once said, "A person's name is to him or her the sweetest and most important sound in any language." Be the person who knows students' names. In some cases, be their "person." One of my favorite television shows was *Grey's Anatomy*. What attracted me most were the relationships among the doctors and how they built those relationships. The first time I heard one doctor say to her friend, "You're my person," I was instantly struck by the emotion I felt. I know that serotonin and oxytocin were released in my brain—the first to calm my body and make me feel good, and the second to make me feel connected to these characters and to remind me who "my person" was at varying times in my life. In an issue of *Educational Leadership* with the theme "What Teens Need from Schools," a column by Fisher and Frey (2019) features a video showing Demetrius Davenport, dean of students at Health Sciences High and Middle College, who clearly is one of those educators who goes out of his way to know all the students' names and tries to speak to them daily.

Pat Wolfe, author of *Brain Matters* (2010), often talked about the "cocktail party effect" during her presentations. This phenomenon refers to the brain's ability to block out chatter in situations such as a cocktail party, where many conversations are occurring at the same time and the brain has the ability to filter out talk that is not important. However, the moment that you hear your name, your brain instantly begins to focus on the conversation that included your name.

This effect has been studied for decades, and as a result neuroscience is getting closer to identifying the exact areas that react to our name being mentioned. The fact is that we are attracted to the sound of our name on many levels. The reticular activating system in the brain stem, which is associated with instincts and controls breathing and other vital functions, responds to our name because survival may be involved. Perhaps our name is going to be followed by a warning to "watch out!" The survival brain does not want to miss the opportunity to save us. And the emotional brain is going to respond to this "name calling" because it may represent the beginning of a compliment, a reprimand, or a pleasurable realization that someone important to you knows your name. Our names are so powerful that even patients in vegetative states show brain activation when their names are spoken (Carmody & Lewis, 2006; NameCoach, 2017). Imagine how important it is for students to hear their own names—pronounced correctly, with a positive connotation! Let's encourage, motivate, and connect with our students in the most basic way by learning and remembering to use their names when speaking to or about them. "Candace, I see that you finished your project, and I can't wait to listen to your presentation!" "Hakim, you look like you have an idea to add to our list. We'd like to hear it!"

Simple statements help us connect to the people around us, so let's use our "name-calling" abilities to build relationships. You will be helping to create a feeling of belonging that can make a world of difference to your students.

Call on Each Student Regularly

If we want to build strong relationships with students, we have to be fair in how we show them that we care. We all have students who want to be called on all the time. They know the answers; they ask the questions. We'd like to have a whole classroom full of "those" kids. And then we have the students who never want to be called on. They may not know the answers, may not be interested, or are just embarrassed to be singled out. So from the beginning, we have to show students that we are trying to be fair. Here are two helpful strategies:

- **Popsicle Stick, or Equity Stick:** Write each student's name on a Popsicle stick, place the sticks in a cup, and draw one name each time you ask a question. Have a second cup to put the sticks in after you ask a question.
- **Stack the Deck:** This strategy involves writing each student's name on an index card. You begin calling on students by picking off the top of the deck each time you ask a question. Once in a while, you can "stack" the deck by putting more than one card in for some students who need the opportunity to speak.

For both these strategies, you may want to drop the stack of cards or spill the Popsicle sticks occasionally. You can then say, "Oops! I guess we're starting over!" Doing this keeps students on their toes even though they have already been called on.

Go the Extra Mile

We can go the extra mile in a number of ways. When I was teaching in high-crime urban areas, it was sometimes scary to attend events in the evening, but together my colleagues and I tried to attend athletic events, debates, reader's theater, and class plays to show our support for our students.

Often when we join a staff at a school, we are asked to take on an extracurricular activity. Doing so can be a great way to build relationships with students. Even if the activity involves only a small number of the students you teach, it's a beginning. Sometimes you may be able to ask students to join your group to let them know that you care and believe in their ability to take on whatever responsibility is involved.

Other ways to go the extra mile include the following:

- Riding the bus with a student who is fearful of other students or doesn't know where to get off
- Sending positive notes home

- Making home visits
- Calling a student after a bad day and discussing it with the parting words "I know tomorrow will be better!"
- Learning an English learner's native language, even if only to speak a small number of common words and phrases.

Try 2 × 10

The 2 × 10 strategy has been used as far back as 1983, when it was introduced by Ray Wlodkowski, and it has become a highly effective teaching practice that appears to work almost universally. The strategy is simple: spend 2 minutes per day for 10 consecutive days talking with an at-risk student about anything the student wants to talk about. Many teachers use this technique with all students. The 2 × 10 strategy takes the pressure off both you and the student. It's a brief intervention for at-risk students and a great relationship-building activity.

This strategy is particularly helpful, according to teachers at all grade levels, in dealing with disruptive students. Practice with one student at a time. Most likely, you will find that after the 10 days, you can have brief positive encounters with that student and maintain a healthy relationship.

Mrs. Walshart has assigned her students to cooperative groups to work on their science project. Avi just couldn't settle down and was interrupting the students in his group as well as students in other groups. Rather than reprimand him (an action that might lead to another struggle), Mrs. Walshart called him up to her desk and began talking to him about what had been going on in his life. Much to her surprise, Avi told her that his father had left home two weeks earlier, his mother was looking for a job, and he (Avi) was in charge of his younger sister both before and after school. It was little wonder that Avi was not himself. After that short, barely two-minute talk, Mrs. Walshart sent Avi back to his group and asked him to listen to his teammates and try to contribute to the project. He did so with no further difficulties that day.

The next day, Mrs. Walshart asked Avi how things were going. He shared a funny story about breakfast being a disaster, as his mom usually fixed wonderful food, and he barely knew how to cook. Mrs. Walshart laughed along with Avi and then offered a brief story of her own. Avi's behavior was much better that day. Mrs. Walshart thought, "Two days down and eight to go!"

Her relationship with Avi and other students improved so much after using the strategy that, whenever she could, Mrs. Walshart took two minutes with other students and improved the overall quality of her relationships with them. Discipline problems were no longer the most important factor in her teaching.

Some teachers say they don't have time to use the strategy—they're seemingly unable to find even two minutes per day to talk to a student. In such cases, I ask if I or someone else can come into the classroom to observe. I know how busy teachers are; I may have said the same thing years ago. When I observe the class, I am focusing on time—our most precious commodity. It never fails that if I am in the class at the right moment, I will see a teacher spending time—from a few seconds to a few minutes—correcting student behavior. I write down the times when this occurs, and after class the teacher and I talk about not only the time spent with the corrections, but also the amount of time needed to get back on task—for both the teacher and the student. Usually it's more than two minutes.

I think many kids desperately want to talk to someone. The first step in the 2 × 10 strategy may be the hardest, and with really tough cases, you may want to start a conversation with a student who likes to speak with you, and do so near the target student. You might even invite that student into the conversation. Remember, it's not a conversation about schoolwork. It's a conversation about getting to know each other.

The following is one of my favorite stories about relationship building, involving a sophomore in my basic English class.

Will was a little bit scary to me. He wore a black leather jacket that he never took off, black pants, black leather boots, and chains of some sort hanging from several pockets. When I tried to engage him in class, he looked at me like... well, like he didn't care for me—or perhaps any other human. He was the only student in my class with whom I could not build rapport. One day, I was walking down the hall and saw Will at his locker. He had earbuds in his ears, and as he turned around, there I was! I think it surprised him. I had been hoping to avoid him; but here we were, face to face, and he looked at me quizzically. I didn't know what to say, but knew I had to say something. I opened with, "Hi, Will! What are you listening to?" It was a rock group—heavy metal, I think—and I had never heard of them. He sort of grunted the name. I responded, "Can I listen?" He took the earbuds out of his ears and offered them to me. They were connected to his phone. I listened for a minute or so; I could barely stand the music. At what I thought was an appropriate time, I took the buds out, smiling all the while, and said, "Cool! Thanks!" He continued to look at me like I might be a bit crazy, so I said, "That brightened my day! I'll see you in class!"

If I told you he magically became a model student after that encounter, I would be lying. But to me it *was* magic, because from that point on, he looked at me with less disdain. He didn't offer to answer questions, nor did he ask any, but he spoke when spoken to. He nodded to me and a few others in the class. It was amazing. I never caught him in the hall again, but when I saw him in the cafeteria (I always make a point of eating in the cafeteria with the students on Fridays—another way to build relationships), we exchanged a few words and sometimes I even got a smile.

Like some other teachers, you may feel that you have nothing in common with some students, but you *do*. You just have to find out what it is. To begin, don't lead with a question. The students who most need the 2 × 10 strategy are often reluctant to answer, and in their experience, teachers do nothing but ask questions. Instead, try to begin with a comment. "My daughter has those jeans! She loves them, and she wears them all the time. I was thinking about getting a pair. Are they comfortable?" Even if I only get a nod in response, I've begun to set something up. Here's another example: "I'm trying to figure out what to get my son for his birthday. Any great ideas come to mind? I was thinking about a _____." Students are almost always responsive to this one. I've shared a little of my life with them this way, and my hope is that with the next encounter, they'll share a little of their life with me. If you have done any "getting to know you" activities (such as "A River Runs Through Us," described on page 34), you may lead with a bit of information you gleaned from those.

Assign Seats

What? How does assigned seating build relationships with students? When students know they have a place in your classroom, that knowledge builds on the idea that they belong somewhere. This is one of those simple background strategies that may be particularly effective with students who find that school is a safer place than home. "My seat. My space. My photos. My cubby. My team." All these possessives may be meaningful to your kids—you know, those kids who become "*my* kids!" You carry them with you in your heart forever—as I do with Will, the "scary" student in my basic English class. He grew up, gave up the motorcycle. (Did I mention the motorcycle? That explains the leather.) He married a niece of one of the teachers. They are living happily ever after.

Schedule Advisories

Advisory class meetings are another way to build relationships, and they're great for all grade levels. Usually scheduled at the beginning of the day, advisory groups at the middle-grade levels then travel together to their classes. The brain loves ritual, and this daily get-together allows students to share their feelings, listen respectfully (an ability that is a characteristic of self-control), and comment in positive ways. Students who are coming from chaotic homes and those who have experienced trauma may find that this is a special place to belong. They have a group in which they can share information with a caring adult who is overseeing the dialogue that takes place. Advisories can have a calming effect and prepare students emotionally for the academic day.

At the high school level, many of the purposes of advisories are the same, but the schedule of the day is, of course, different. Advisory purposes can be academic, motivational, relational, to plan a learning pathway, to discuss post–high school plans, or simply to help students feel included and accepted. This may be a time for students to share thoughts and concerns or perhaps compliments. Everyday advisories are ideal, but scheduling them for twice a week will work, too. Here are some ideas for how to fit an advisory meeting into the day:

- Use homeroom time.
- Find time during the lunch period (see "Form a Lunch Bunch" on page 35).
- Choose a time normally used for classroom routines.
- Schedule time as necessary. (If my homeroom time wasn't enough, we met at lunchtime, too.)

Conduct Morning Meetings

Morning meetings are a wonderful way to build community in a classroom. Generally considered a gathering for lower grades, many schools find the meetings rewarding and use them throughout the grades. Here are the typical components of a morning meeting:

- **Greeting:** Even though you have already greeted your students at the door, the meeting is a great way to greet them again and offer a welcome to the day.
- **Sharing:** Students have an opportunity to share something in their lives and give classmates a chance to ask questions.
- **Group activity:** The beginning of the year is a great time for a "getting to know each other" activity. My favorite is "A River Runs Through Us," which was introduced to me decades ago at a workshop I attended. I have used it in my classrooms and my workshops ever since. Here are the steps:

  1. Chairs are arranged in a tight circle, with no spaces in between.
  2. Students sit in the chairs, and the teacher stands in the middle of the circle.
  3. The teacher begins with, "Hi, I'm Miss (or Ms., Mr., Mrs.) _____."
  4. Students respond with, "Hi, Miss _____."
  5. The teacher continues with personal content, such as "I have a dog... and a river runs through us."
  6. At this point, all students who also have a dog must get up from their seat and find an open seat to sit in. At the same time, the teacher tries to grab a seat.
  7. The person left standing goes to the middle, introduces herself, and makes a statement.

Students at all grade levels enjoy this activity. We play until I am sure all students have been in the middle and shared something about themselves. By the time the activity is over, I know everyone's name and some things we have in common, making future interactions (like 2 × 10) much easier.

- **Announcements:** This segment could include mention of special events like an assembly or anything else that has come up and needs to be shared.

Form a Lunch Bunch

Many middle and high schools don't allow enough time for a morning meeting. Schedules can be tight, and classes may be short. As an alternative, meeting for a few minutes at lunch or having lunch with students has worked well at some schools. As a middle school teacher, I had a very short homeroom period. As I mentioned previously, I ate lunch in the cafeteria with my students on Fridays. Doing so gave me a chance to check in with them to find out who was looking forward to the weekend, how they felt about their class work or assessments that week, and whether they needed to talk later about anything specific. It was really one of the best opportunities for me to connect with my students.

Nurture Relationships

Cook and his colleagues (2018) at the University of Minnesota conducted a study of classrooms in which teachers used a series of techniques centered on establishing, maintaining, and restoring relationships. The original study was done with 220 4th and 5th graders, and it was repeated with middle school students. The results showed that academic engagement increased by 33 percent and disruptive behavior decreased by 75 percent—outcomes that resulted in more quality, uninterrupted classroom time. The establish-maintain-restore (EMR) method breaks relationships into three steps: starting and establishing, maintenance to avoid deterioration, and repair to fix any breakdown. Strategies recommended at each step include the following:

Starting and Establishing
- Offer positive greetings at the door (as described in this chapter).
- Ask open-ended and reflective questions.
- Incorporate student-led activities.
- Make time for one-on-one encounters (as in the 2 × 10 strategy).

Maintenance
- Check in with students regularly.
- Recognize good behavior.
- Keep interactions positive.

I like to add Stephen Covey's ways to make deposits in emotional bank accounts:
- Keep commitments.
- Attend to the little things.
- Clarify expectations.

Repairing and Restoring
- Avoid holding mistakes over students' heads.
- Criticize behavior, not the student.
- Take responsibility for your part of the problem.
- Work with those affected—face up.
- Make things right—fix up.
- Change behavior—follow up.

The process of relationship building, maintaining, and repairing comes in many different forms. Letting students get to know you is the first step.

Every Student Has a Story

Sarah, the teacher in the opening scenario, tried many of the strategies discussed in this chapter. She found the 2 × 10 strategy to be very effective. Even with 150 students, she found that kids talk, and as she spent those few minutes each day with one student, that student told his friends. The perception of her not caring changed.

We live our lives in relationships. As we work with students, sometimes it's hard to remember that they are not there to *give us* a hard time; rather, *they are having* a hard time. Some of them have come from situations that have wired their brains for stress. They may perceive new and unfamiliar situations as a threat. All students need is one caring adult in their lives to make a difference. We need to know and use positive ways to respond when addressing situations. The following are some if/then statements to consider.

If...	Then...
You want to build relationships,	Build trust, speak respectfully, and call students by name.
You want to build trust,	Make eye contact, follow through, use their names, and go the extra mile.
You want to improve behavior,	Use the relationship you have to speak to students, create a contract, or say something like "That's not the behavior I see from _____ [insert name]. The _____ I know is kind. Is there something you want to tell me?"
You want to improve academic achievement,	Make students feel that they belong.
You need to repair relationships,	Take responsibility for your part in the breakdown.

If...	Then...
You want students to feel like they belong,	Show each child that you respect them as well as like them and their differences.
You need to start at the beginning with a student,	Start with a smile, add a greeting, and share your own story.

2

Empathy

Empathy can be cultivated, and doing so transforms our children's lives.

—Michele Borba

Elsie walked into the classroom, threw her books down on the desk, and, with tears in her eyes, said, "Everyone laughed at me when I said I was going to try out for cheerleading. They said I couldn't jump up and down without falling. And Briana said, 'Cheerleaders don't wear their hair like you do. And they wear cool clothes. Try out for band.' Then everyone laughed some more."

In a scenario like this, my brain wants to react impulsively rather than reflectively. My first thought is "Let's get those girls!" But, of course, a teacher can't do that. As I look at Elsie, I wonder if I should just tell her to toughen up. Middle school is a microcosm of real life. Buck up! There will be people in your life who will love you, and there will be people who won't. What's more, there will be those whom you want to laugh at and throw out of your life. But this is not the time to take this approach.

Teachers who really love their students and care for their well-being may respond in such situations by saying something like "I really liked the sweater you wore yesterday" or "Maybe you could wear your hair down like you did last year." Are these examples of showing empathy? No. Statements like these actually show your agreement with the "everyone" Elsie is talking about.

Being an empathic teacher means going deep inside yourself and finding that place that allows you to relate to someone else. At one time, we were all sweaty-palmed, insecure 7th graders. The empathic teacher might say, "I'm sorry. I know this hurts." The empathic teacher does not promise to punish the offenders, does not offer advice on fashion or hair. The empathic teacher sits with Elsie and acknowledges her feelings—and lets her know she belongs.

You can't be empathic without being vulnerable. You can't put yourself in someone's shoes without exposing yourself and the person with whom you empathize to your authentic self. Kids try their best to do one of two things: fit in or belong. There is a huge difference between the two. "Fitting in" is about changing yourself to be like others, but "belonging" is being who you are without fear of ridicule or embarrassment, without having to change (Brown, 2018).

I Feel Your Pain

"Empathy is caught, not taught," says author and researcher Mary Gordon (2009). Many of us lament the fact that our students don't come to school with empathic tendencies. We wish so much that empathy was modeled at home. In *Born for Love,* Szalavitz and Perry (2010) state, "Empathy isn't extended to everyone. And certain specific experiences, certain particular actions on the part of those closest to us, are required for empathy to develop in children"

(p. 3). But if empathy isn't modeled, how are students to become empathic?

Mary Gordon started the Roots of Empathy program in 1996. This highly effective method of developing empathy in schoolchildren is endorsed by two esteemed researchers, Bruce Perry and Michelle Borba. In their best-selling books, they each explain the difference that Roots of Empathy makes in the classroom. Gordon's idea was to bring a baby into the classroom once a month. The students observe, encourage, and discuss what the baby is feeling. They watch the baby grow and change and predict how the baby is feeling based on their observations of body language, facial expression, and actions the baby takes. The metaphor for empathy that Gordon used in an interview was "breathing with the same lung as somebody else" (2010).

Some research suggests that our affluent students, in particular, lack empathy (Gregoire, 2018; Grewal, 2012). That is, in general, richer people tend to think less often of others; they are not in tune with the suffering of other people. I have seen this phenomenon play out in schools throughout the United States. Students who have socioeconomic benefits often do not respond empathically to others less fortunate. Of course, this does not pertain to all children from wealthy households. It depends on whether or how empathy was shown by their caregivers.

Some students don't show empathy because they are so unaccustomed to dire circumstances that they succumb to avoidance—for instance, avoiding a friend who is suffering over the death of a parent. Rather than empathize, the student avoids her friend. You have probably seen or experienced this situation yourself. You or a family member becomes critically ill. Some friends stay close and jump in to help, while others keep their distance.

We might think that we find out who our true friends are under these circumstances, but actually some powerful neurobiology is involved in the differing responses. Empathy can cause pain. For instance, I am an animal lover, and when I see a TV commercial showing abused animals and dogs in puppy mills, I change the channel. It literally pains me to watch those commercials. I am not drawn to action. I do not send money to the organization, perhaps because I am skeptical that the money will really help the dogs. I also know that donating to the organization is not going to relieve the pain I feel. I know the donation isn't enough to right the wrong.

Types of Empathy

Some people call the ability to be empathic "mindsight," indicating an ability to know the minds both of others and of ourselves. Author and lecturer Stephen Covey (2015) wrote, "Seek first to understand, then to be understood" (p. 247). I think this is especially relevant for educators. Our job is to impart knowledge as well as to help students explore and discover. We are constantly trying to be understood. However, as John Hattie's (2012) research shows, an empathic teacher has empathy for each student and knows *how* each student learns. The starting point is empathy—understanding where each student resides in the learning of the content.

Empathy can be classified into three types: cognitive empathy, emotional empathy, and compassionate empathy, suggesting a spectrum of seeing, feeling, and caring for others. Let's take a closer look at the types of empathy and consider where our teaching falls within this spectrum.

Cognitive empathy, also known as perspective taking, is the ability to understand how a person feels and what they may be thinking. Listening is key here. In order to understand, communication must be clear. The vocabulary that students may use can inform the type of response we give in order to truly reach them.

Emotional empathy is affective. It is the ability to actually share the feelings of another. With this type of empathy, we build emotional connections. The other person feels "felt."

Compassionate empathy, also called empathic concern, takes us beyond the first two types of understanding and sharing. With compassionate empathy, we are moved to action. We try to help.

To illustrate the three types of empathy, consider this scenario. Your student arrives at school in tears. You hear through other students that the family had to take their dog to the vet to be euthanized. You may, at first, sympathize and tell the student how sorry you are as you greet him at the door. If you want to show empathy, however, you must make more of an effort. You may first imagine what the student is experiencing (cognitive empathy). You may wonder how long the student's family had the dog and how close the student was to the dog. Emotional empathy takes you to a level of trying to connect the student's experience to your own. Perhaps you lost a pet at some point in your life and you remember how it felt, or you just try to imagine how it would feel. Finally, compassionate empathy makes you take action. You may spend some extra time with the student if he wants to talk, or give him a place to be alone. If he is terribly upset, you may excuse him from an assignment until he feels more composed. If he wants to be distracted, you may choose a group activity that will preoccupy him. All these options show compassion—and the pathway to that compassion is empathy.

Empathy in the Brain

In a 2013 study from the Max Planck Institutes, researchers discovered that a part of our brain corrects us when we are too egocentric and not empathic. This structure, the *right supramarginal gyrus,* is in the frontal lobe of the brain, at the point where this lobe connects to the parietal and temporal lobes (Silani, Lamm, Ruff, & Singer,

2013). The finding suggests that the supramarginal gyrus allows our brain to "autocorrect"—that is, it directs us to other individuals and allows us to "walk in their shoes." (See Figure 2.1.)

Figure 2.1
Empathy in the Brain

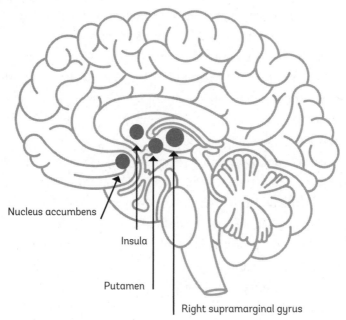

"When the right supramarginal gyrus doesn't perform properly—or, as in the case of children, when it hasn't had time to develop—a person is more likely to project his own feelings and circumstances onto others" (Siegel & Bryson, 2018, p. 146). The good news is that the supramarginal gyrus continues to develop as children mature, and the more they use it, the better it works.

The results of a study from the University of Virginia (Coan, Becks, & Hasselmo, 2013) suggest that we are powerfully hardwired to empathize because we closely associate those people who are close to us (e.g., spouses, friends, partners) with ourselves. The ego-centricity that we all experience is natural. We are supposed to put ourselves first as a survival mechanism. When we let others get close to us, that sense of who we are and who they are comes together in the brain.

Coan and colleagues (2013) used *functional magnetic resonance imaging* (fMRI) brain scans to discover that we closely relate to people to whom we are attached. In other words, our self-identity is mostly based on whom we know and with whom we empathize. In addition to the *supramarginal gyrus,* the parts of the brain that are activated when we relate to people we know and to whom we feel close are the *anterior insula* and the *putamen* (see Figure 2.1). These three areas are not activated by strangers. When we *do* feel empathy for strangers, it is most likely because of some common thread. For instance, when we think of the terrorist attacks of September 11, 2001, we may recall that the pain and death of complete strangers touched us and we empathized with the families who lost members, the firefighters who courageously helped victims, and other first responders. Most people felt a kinship during this event; we became one, a world of humans. Our very first thoughts may have been for ourselves and our families and friends, but as the ordeal unfolded, our *mirror neuron* system kicked in as we projected ourselves into the tragic situation and felt others' pain.

Mirror neurons scattered throughout the brain fire when we perform an action and when we see someone else perform it. Current research supports the theory that mirror neurons also fire when individuals observe the emotions of others. The firing action helps us "feel" what someone else is experiencing on some level, even if we're not experiencing it directly. If we share someone's joy, neurons in the emotional center, especially the *nucleus accumbens,* the pleasure center, are activated in our brains as well as in the brains of those actually experiencing the joy firsthand. Similarly, fear will awaken our amygdala just as it is awakened in the person who has the fear. Think about the student in your class who has high test anxiety. If you can relate to this experience because you also had test anxiety, you may be more empathic. You may do whatever you can to help the student overcome that anxiety. In the situation of friends avoiding you mentioned earlier, it may be that the pain you are experiencing is so great that your friends actually feel it as well and it becomes overwhelming, leading them to stay away. When any of our loved ones are in pain, it may be very difficult for us to be happy. I have always told my friends, "You are only as happy as your unhappiest child." Or perhaps you've heard the expression "If Mama ain't happy, ain't nobody happy." Is it because Mama will make everyone miserable if she is unhappy, or is it that we feel her pain?

According to John Medina (2018), we actually recruit these mirror neuron systems when we share an experience. They are activated along with our emotional system and our memory systems, all working together to help us understand and relate to the occurrence taking place.

Strategies for Developing Empathy

Infants show empathy in a nursery when they join other babies in crying. Toddlers show empathy when they try to stop another toddler, a sibling, or a parent from crying by distracting them, talking to them, or simply being sad right along with them. What can possibly be done in the classroom to teach empathy to a child who has already had the experience of showing empathy? When some of our students reach a certain age or become part of a situation in which empathy is not shown or allowed, the memory of those experiences may fade. We need strategies to remind those who have previously experienced empathy what it looked and felt like, as well as to educate those who have not had the experience at all. Following are strategies that have been used by educators to "teach" empathy.

Modeling

Modeling is possibly the number one strategy for teaching empathy. Your students watch what you do. Just as young children carefully watch their parents' reactions and interactions, all students watch their teachers—especially during interactions with another student. If a student did something right, others want to see how you treat that student. If a student did something wrong, others want to see how you look at and speak to that student and how you respond in general to the situation. Students are curious to see how you will treat them if they are in a similar situation. They are very aware of how you treat them and others when they are angry, upset, or frustrated. When you try to understand them and make them feel safe and loved, they may share their feelings more readily.

Angel was no angel. He always came to school late and almost never had his homework done. His 6th grade teachers were frustrated and a bit angry because they wanted a future for Angel that would get him out of the neighborhood in which he lived with his mother and sisters.

What the teachers didn't know was that although Angel was the youngest in the family, in his culture, all women were revered. Therefore, it was his duty to listen to whatever the women in the house said and do whatever they asked. He was the man of the family, as his dad rarely made an appearance. As a result, Angel needed to fill the void. He was so busy pleasing his mother and sisters, he rarely got to do anything for himself.

One morning, two of his teachers, Mrs. Miller and Mrs. McGraw, "cornered" Angel in the hallway.

Mrs. Miller: "Angel, you're late again. How do you get to school?"

Angel: "I run, Mrs. Miller. I run!"

Mrs. McGraw: "Why do you leave so late that you have to run?"

Angel: "If I don't do the breakfast dishes before I leave, my mom has to do them, and she doesn't always feel so good in the mornings. Her bones hurt."

Mrs. Miller: "Angel, all the schools have breakfast programs for every student. Have you thought about that?"

Angel: "I don't know if my sisters would eat breakfast at school. They are pretty fussy. They make pancakes and eggs and sometimes bacon. Do you know how messy bacon grease is? And how hard it is to clean?"

Mrs. McGraw: "Angel, we would really like to help. How about if we talk to your mom about school breakfast—and about how important it is for you to get to school on time and have time to do your homework?"

Angel: "I don't know if that will work. I don't want my dad to get mad at me for not taking care of the family."

The teachers called Mrs. Menendez and made an appointment to see her and Angel's sisters at their home. They explained how much potential Angel had, how he needed time to do his work, and the importance of getting to school on time. Not one of the females in the house wanted to hold Angel back from a good future. An agreement was made to have elaborate breakfasts on the weekend and to take turns cleaning the kitchen each morning. The teachers knew that Angel might be late on Tuesdays because that was his morning to clean, but the girls agreed to have frozen waffles and cereal on his day.

Angel was almost never late again, and the encouragement and empathy he felt from his teachers made it easier for him to work harder both at school and on homework. When Angel had issues with content or with personal situations, he had two people at school in his corner that he could count on. The other students in the school knew that they would also be treated with compassion, and they began to trust the teachers more.

Seeking to Understand

Empathy, which begins with attempting to see something from another's perspective or point of view, is not always an easy task, so be upfront and ask the right questions. Karyn Gordon (2012) suggests that we ask, "Can you help me understand how you see this?" Although at first a student may have difficulty answering this question, just the fact that you care enough to ask may help lower the student's stress and make it easier to trust and share with you.

"Ask, Don't Tell"

Karyn Gordon (Beach, 2010) believes the "ask, don't tell" approach is very important. We all have a tendency to *tell* kids how they are feeling. We mean well when we say things like "You must be sad about . . ." or "You look angry. . . ." Some researchers (Barrett, 2018) question how much we can rely on facial expressions and body language. It makes more sense to be cautious and ask or say, "I imagine that you feel _____. Am I right?" or "Could you tell me how you feel?"

Notes of Appreciation

You know all those appreciation days we try to do at school: Teacher Appreciation Day, Custodian Appreciation Day, and so on? Sometimes we don't appreciate appropriately. We need to involve students. So how about a bulletin board or table dedicated to thanking the people who do things for us? My cheerleaders loved to have pep assemblies for appreciation days, but time constraints made it difficult. So they created a table with a sign saying, "Two, Four, Six, Eight, Who Do WE Appreciate?" Beneath this would go the person's name or a category. For instance, during Cafeteria Workers Week, the students could write a group note or individual notes if someone had done something specifically helpful to them. Brightly colored notes and small notes with envelopes were available. Students could stop by, write a thank-you note, and know it was going to be delivered to the appropriate person during their appreciation day or week. We displayed posters with the names of potential recipients so students would be sure to spell the names correctly. (We added that after a disappointed custodian received a thank-you note with her name misspelled.)

A Kindness Wall

Encourage kindness with bulletin boards and sticky notes displayed in the hall, the library, or any convenient spot where students gather. A collage of kindness is an impressive display. The sticky notes and pens are attached to the board with a question such as "What kind act did you see or do today?" Notes appear quickly as students think about incidents at school that were kind acts. The observations may be as simple as "Sarah held the door for Mr. Knox" or "Milo carried Sasha's books today because her wrist is sprained." Students are asked to "pay it forward" if they received a kind act. Doing so encourages more kindness.

I always ask myself when I suggest these sorts of kindness activities, "Would adolescents do this?" Some schools find that if the sticky notes are available, adolescents will spread kindness like confetti, according to journalist Kerri Beauchesne (2018), writing in *PTO Today*. Posting anonymous notes on kindness walls—or on places such as lockers and cars—can make teens more aware of kindness. They often think something is nice but don't express it at the time. Kindness activities provide an opportunity to "catch up" on kindness.

Face-to-Face Conversations

According to Michele Borba (2016), having face-to-face conversations is the best way to build empathy. There is some research suggesting that kids can develop empathy via social media and other online means, but it is important to limit variables and circumstances when students are first learning about empathy, with you as their coach. Why? Trying to understand the context that shapes the intent of the written word is difficult at best. Some studies have indicated that students who disengage from "screen time" for several days show a better understanding of emotional cues and stronger empathic responses (Uhls et al., 2014). Face-to-face communication conveys social information via a multitude of vocal and visual cues within the context of the situation. Nonverbal communication includes apparent behaviors such as facial expression, eye contact, and tone of voice, as well as less obvious messages such as posture and spatial distance between two or more people (Knapp & Hall, 2010).

Because most schools do not allow students to use personal devices during class time, these times are ideal for helping students become skilled at face-to-face conversations. Here are some ideas:

- To help students become comfortable with eye contact, tell them to look at the color of the speaker's eyes. Watching for visual cues and facial expressions will be easier if they focus on the eyes.
- Borba (2016) suggests using fun "staring contests" to get students comfortable with looking someone straight in the eyes. My middle schoolers love these contests, which are easy to do when you have just a minute or two of downtime between activities.
- Hit the pause button. Tell students that everything gets put on pause when they are having a one-on-one conversation.

Community Service Projects

Armstrong (2019) suggests getting students involved in community projects such as conducting food drives, visiting nursing homes to engage with senior citizens who may appreciate having someone to talk to, helping after disasters, or assisting with city beautification through picking up litter. Identifying city and community needs may challenge students to do some research that will require both cognitive and SEL abilities. And involving your whole class—including students who don't always show compassion—expands student engagement beyond members of the student council and other groups or organizations that might typically undertake such activities.

Volunteer Work

Volunteer work may include helping in the school library or cafeteria as well as at outside establishments. You can ask for volunteers to create bulletin boards or to welcome a new student to class. When guests are coming to visit your classroom, ask for volunteers to greet them, get them anything they need, and explain what is going on in the classroom.

Classroom Pets

A hamster named Homey was our class pet when I was teaching 7th grade in an inner-city school. I was amazed how his presence made a difference in the lives of so many of my "tough" students who otherwise rarely showed emotion, compassion, or empathy. Many would hold the hamster and stroke him, and the most unlikely students volunteered to care for our pet, from feeding him to cleaning the cage and then just holding him. Similar to the behaviors displayed in the Roots of Empathy program described earlier, my students discussed whether Homey was hungry or lonely. Obviously, the hamster didn't have facial expressions the students could read, but it was possible for them to interpret body language. Most notable, however, was how the students used Homey to help other students. I would hear, for example, "Mrs. S., Jada is sad. Maybe if she held Homey for a while, she'd feel better."

Pet ownership brings with it a multitude of responsibilities, but it also brings opportunities. Interaction with school therapy dogs (discussed further in Chapter 4) has been shown to calm students, lower blood pressure, help with pain management, and reduce stress. Giving students the opportunity to interact with the dogs also brings out some empathic responses as the kids relate to and care for the animal. Improved test scores are another positive "side effect" (Zalanick, 2019).

Mix-It-Up-at-Lunch Day

This strategy, created by the organization Teaching Tolerance (Teaching Tolerance Staff, 2019) as an international campaign that millions of kids participate in simultaneously, simply involves sitting with someone you don't know in the cafeteria. The date is usually in October, but you can designate any day or multiple days throughout the year. Organizing the activity can be as simple as giving students color-coded ribbons to designate their lunch-table group, decorating the cafeteria in a festive way, and placing some conversation starters on the tables. Students at all levels will tell you that the cafeteria is the place where distinct lines are drawn between kids, and many are very uncomfortable at lunchtime. Mixing it up at lunch can help improve the situation. The Teaching Tolerance website has resources and ideas for this strategy (https://www .tolerance.org/magazine/what-is-mix-it-up-at-lunch).

Literature

As a literature teacher for decades, I found that teaching components of SEL was somewhat easier during literature lessons than in some of my other content areas. Students could relate to and empa-thize with characters in books and stories. Research now supports the use of literature to help students understand, identify with, and feel for and with characters and situations. Reading literary fiction enhances the ability to connect with others and empathize. Accord-ing to Kidd and Castano (2013), great writers provide incomplete characters and compel readers to try to understand what is going on inside those characters' heads; fiction in which readers must partici-pate rather than just be entertained encourages this understanding. Other studies have shown that reading literary fiction can prompt personality changes that include improvements in empathic ability (Djikic & Oatley, 2014). Literature immerses readers in a simulated social world in which they interact with others, which can change how they see themselves. In other words, literature can figuratively cause students to walk in someone else's shoes.

Even simple stories like "The Three Little Pigs" or "Little Red Riding Hood" can produce these effects. Asking students to change their points of view and look at either story from the wolf's per-spective can be a starting point for students to change perspectives. Works by Charles Dickens and Jane Austen were found to elicit an empathy effect when volunteers underwent brain scans while reading them. *To Kill a Mockingbird* and *Charlotte's Web* may cause us to wince, cry, or grit our teeth as we try to figure out the inten-tions or emotions of characters and are compelled to step into their shoes. Many kids can relate to *Ramona the Pest* as Ramona becomes an unforgettable part of their lives (Borba, 2016).

Epiphany in a Brown Paper Bag

Michele Borba (2016) says that empathy can bullyproof our classrooms. While conducting research for this book, I ran across an article titled "Bullyproof Your Classroom with Brown Paper Bags," by teacher Maggie Grate (2014), that seems to confirm Borba's conclusion. Grate developed a strategy with the help of others called "Epiphany in a Paper Bag" (I love the name, and it kept me reading). She gave each student three green and three pink sticky notes. On the green notes, each student was asked to write three things other students had done to make them feel happy or special, fold the notes, and write the name of the student responsible on the outside. Grate had the students follow the same procedure with the pink notes but to write something that happened that made them feel upset, embarrassed, or angry. She prepared a brown paper sack for each student with their name on it, collected the notes, and placed the correct notes in each student's bag. After distributing the bags, she gave the students time to look through the notes they had received. Some students had exclusively pink notes in their bags, some had only green notes, and most had a mixture. After the students had the opportunity to read the notes—and some had a lot of notes to read—a large-group discussion followed. This was an opportunity for students to see the impact they had on others. Students who had caused their classmates pain were surprised and remorseful. Other students offered suggestions as to how to handle certain situations. Students who were always nice shared their feelings about the difficulty of maintaining this behavior. The entire discussion gave students the opportunity to empathize with classmates, and the activity changed the climate in the classroom. This seems to be an idea worth spreading!

Crumpled Hearts

Another anti-bullying activity, developed by the Ripple Kindness Project (2019), can help students understand the damage that bullying can do. Suitable for any age level, it emphasizes the importance of empathy and kindness. After giving each student a red paper heart, follow these steps:

1. Ask students to look at how beautiful and perfect their heart is. Now ask them to imagine that this is their own, real heart and to give it to the student standing next to them, [asking that person] to love and care for their heart as they hand it over.

2. Ask each student to say mean things to the heart they were just given and to crumple it up into a tight little ball, throw it on the ground, and stomp on it.

3. Have students pick up the crumpled little ball, look at the student who owns the heart, and say they're sorry. Turn their attention back to the student's heart (paper ball) and apologize, say they didn't mean to be so thoughtless, they really didn't know what came over them and could [the owner] forgive them. While [students are] apologizing, [have them] carefully uncrumple the heart, place it on a table, and try to smooth it out [as much as possible].

4. [Have] students return hearts to their owners. Each person holds up their crumpled heart. Ask them how it looks now. Is it still perfect? Did the person they gave it to care for it?

5. Explain that every time a person hurls abuse, belittles, talks behind someone's back, bullies, writes unkind things on social media, etc., they are responsible for adding a crinkle to that person's heart.

6. Even though they may apologize later, that crinkle cannot be smoothed out. Sure, it may fade over time, but that person's heart will never really be the same and the scars will remain for a lifetime.

7. Take the opportunity to talk about the responsibility we all have to care for other people and their feelings. (https://ripplekindness.org/crumpled-paper-bullying-exercise/)

Teacher Self-Assessment

Ask yourself, "Am I empathic when I am interacting with my students?" Perhaps you've never thought about the fact that empathy can be a factor in every encounter you have with students. For years, I have been explaining to teachers that they change students' brains every day, but I didn't stop to think about how hard our own brains are working, including when we are expressing empathy.

Researcher Helen Riess (2018) suggests three questions to ask ourselves if we truly want to become more empathic:

- **What is this person feeling?** To find the answer to this question, become a good listener as well as an observer. Body language, tone of voice, and facial expressions can offer some clues. But be sure to ask questions to discover exactly what is going on from the other person's perspective. Be sure to remain open, make eye contact, and use a soothing tone.
- **Have I ever felt this way?** Once you have a handle on what the other person is feeling, think about a time when you may have felt the same way. No matter the difference in age, gender, or experience, the human condition allows for all of us to have similar feelings about diverse experiences. Dig deep to relate to the feelings.
- **How would I want to be treated if I felt this way?** The Golden Rule pops up for this question. Even if you don't have the same experience, imagine yourself in this situation. Treating others with kindness, respect, love, and compassion will help you build the trust they will need to provide you with more information and create a relationship that will eventually enable you to more specifically give them what they need.

Consider the following situations.

Situation #1 may be your first eye contact with a student. Whether it is your morning greeting or a normal encounter during the day, you do some mind reading: *How is he doing? Does she look upset? Where did he get that bruise on his face?* Your first empathic moment is when you switch from the natural egocentricity bias that puts us in the pattern of thinking, "Doesn't everyone see the world my way?" (Siegel & Bryson, 2018) to an authentic demonstration of empathy. (Remember, what gets us there is the supramarginal gyrus.)

Situation #2 is quite possibly your interaction with students in your classroom. In this case, switching from egocentricity to being empathic is more difficult; after all, you are providing a wonderful lesson that you have carefully and craftily designed to reach your learners. When students do not understand the concept, the process, or the instructions, the urge to "say it louder and slower" is our brain's way of saying, "Hey, I put this together so you would understand. So *understand!*" Enter empathy. Where is the student coming from? According to Hattie (2012), "The essence of the student-centered teacher is fourfold: a student-centered teacher has warmth, trust, empathy, and positive relationship" (p. 158). The teacher must try to see the lesson from the student's point of view. Understanding the student's situation aids in assisting that student.

Here's an example from my own experience. When Akio showed up late to class and hadn't read the assignment, I wanted to ask, "What is wrong with you?" But I am so grateful I did not, because when I said, "Akio, you are usually prompt and on top of your work; is there something wrong?" Akio replied, "No, Mrs. Sprenger. I was up till midnight at the laundromat doing the kids' [his younger siblings'] clothes so they'd have something to wear today. I tried to read while I waited for the clothes to get done, but those machines make a lot of noise!" That response certainly changed my approach. Before anything else, I offered to let him sleep in the nurse's office, which he did for two hours!

Granted, this was an extreme case. Often, the issues our students have relate more to their learning preferences. They require a different approach to understand, appreciate, and even become passionate about a subject. Teachers need to be "adaptive learning experts" (Hattie, 2012).

Situation #3 often occurs because of inappropriate behavior. This kind of situation calls for an empathic mindset. Rather than treating the behavior punitively, teachers with this mindset treat students with empathy and compassion. Researchers from Stanford (Parker, 2016) conducted three separate studies involving teachers from different content areas and students from ethnically diverse backgrounds. Teachers were asked to write about how "good teacher-student relationships are critical for students to learn self-control" (an empathic mindset) or how "punishment is critical for teachers to take control of the classroom" (a punitive mindset). "The findings showed that giving teachers an opportunity to express their empathic values—to understand students' perspectives and to sustain positive relationships with students when they misbehave—improved student-teacher relationships and discipline outcomes" (p. 1). Teachers given the punitive-mindset task offered harsher punishment for hypothetical students. Keeping in mind the information in Chapter 1 on relationships and how empathy can change outcomes for students, it is easy to see how empathy leads to a happier classroom and a happier you!

Every Student Has a Story

Empathy is the glue of relationships and is so important in our interactions with students. Some may be dealing with trauma, and if they reach out to us, what we say matters. Most students need empathy to deal with things that we may not consider to be a problem. "This too shall pass" is a common response to students whose issue we, as adults, know is temporary. But if we want to keep our relationships strong to help improve everything from behavior to academic performance, we need to start saying the right thing. What we say could make or break our relationship with a student, and repairing relationships takes time that could be spent in other ways.

As you interact with students to model empathy, try to make statements that show empathy. Consider the examples in the following if/then table.

If a student says...	Instead of saying...	Say this...
"I failed my science test."	"How much did you study?"	"That really sucks! I'm sorry to hear that."
"My friends won't sit with me at lunch."	"I remember when my friends did the same thing to me."	"I'm sorry you're going through this."
"My mom and dad are getting a divorce."	"This could be a blessing in disguise."	"I can see how this will be difficult."
"My grandpa is dying."	"It's the circle of life."	"My heart hurts for you."
"No one wants to be my friend."	"What did you do?"	"That must be hard for you."
"My dad went to prison."	"Maybe he will change there."	"I can't imagine what you are going through."
"I let my dog out, and she didn't come home last night."	"Don't you have a fenced-in yard?"	"Our pets are family. It makes me really sad to hear that this happened."

3.

Self-Awareness

If you feel safe and loved, your brain becomes specialized in exploration, play, and cooperation; if you are frightened and unwanted, it specializes in managing feelings of fear and abandonment.

—Bessel van der Kolk

Identical twin sisters Jane and Joan marry identical twin brothers Rob and Rich. They are happily married young couples. They all have good jobs and are moving up in their careers. Jane is driven to become CEO of her company; work is the most important thing to her. Her coworkers like her, her supervisors like her, and she is on the fast track to success. Joan loves her work as well. She is not as competitive or driven as her sister, but she is happy with her life.

Both sisters become pregnant at the same time, unintentionally. This is not the time in their lives that they had planned for babies, but up to now they have done everything together successfully, so they figure this is just another challenge. Neither sister is an enthusiastic mother-to-be. After baby showers given by their coworkers, baby items are decorating the nursery in Joan's house; Jane has everything neatly stacked, still in boxes.

No, they didn't give birth on the same day, nor did they have twins. But each had a boy. Think about it: these boys have the same DNA! Jane and Rob named their son Jason, and Joan and Rich named their son Ricky.

Here is where their stories diverge more significantly. Jane rarely smiles at Jason. She wishes she were back at work instead of on maternity leave. She arranges to work remotely from home during the rest of her leave. When Jason cries in his crib, Jane doesn't go to him because, in her words, "I won't be manipulated by a baby!" As Jason grows and becomes curious, Jane tells him his questions are stupid and to speak only when spoken to, and she punishes him for interrupting her when she is on the phone.

Joan, by contrast, falls in love with her baby boy. She smiles at Ricky, takes him for walks, and talks to him throughout the day, whether changing his diaper or fixing dinner. She loves to sing to him, and he often tries to coo along. When Ricky becomes a toddler and begins to ask questions, Joan typically replies by saying, "What a good question! I don't know the answer, so let's go look it up together." When Joan is on the phone and Ricky needs her, he has been taught to say, "Excuse me, Mommy!"

Soon the two boys are old enough to start school. There is only one kindergarten classroom, and the teacher speaks very fast. Because Ricky has been exposed to rich language, he understands and gets to work. If he has a question, he has no problem asking for help. Jason, on the other hand, can't keep up with what the teacher is telling him, but he would never think to ask a "stupid" question. He sits there and does nothing. The teacher doesn't notice, given all the commotion going on in the room.

When students walk into the classroom, backpacks and textbooks aren't the only baggage they bring with them. Everyone enters the room in a different mental, emotional, and physical state, which often affects their readiness and willingness to learn. The way children have been treated early in life determines how they feel about themselves. What can be frustrating for both students and teachers is an inability to identify how the student is actually feeling. In the case of Jason, he feels inadequate and fears humiliation; almost any social situation is difficult for him. Yet he is unable to label or express his feelings because he has been told much of what he feels is wrong.

Students who act out in class are doing so because of a "feeling" they have. We need to help them name that feeling or emotion. Emotions—including those we are unaware of—dictate behaviors, some of which may be inappropriate. Self-awareness is the ability to recognize our own emotions in various situations and to put a name to them. This ability is a result of others having recognized those emotions and having helped us label them. ("You look sad. I'm so sorry that you lost your doll.")

Emotional coaching is time consuming and energy zapping, but it's part of what teaching is about these days. Unfortunately, not all parents are equipped to be emotional coaches, and we have the opportunity to help as we spend so much time with their children. We can begin by helping students recognize their emotions so they can learn to control them. Once these emotions are controlled, students are capable of recognizing the emotions of others.

It is common for adults and kids alike to say they are "stressed." Often the term *stress* is used to describe several different emotions: anxiety, fear, pressure, and actual stress. However, there are differences among these four. *Anxiety* is worry about a future uncertainty that we feel we cannot control. *Fear* is a sense of upcoming danger. *Pressure* is an outside force telling us that if we don't do something well, we may fail. *Stress* is a combination of these: we are anxious and fearful that we won't be able to handle the pressure from all that is demanded of us (Brackett, 2019). So you can see that the more granular we get when describing emotions, the easier it will be to get the help we need.

CASEL (2017) pinpoints the following competencies as components of self-awareness:

- **Be able to identify emotions.** Self-awareness begins with students' ability to name or label their own emotions.
- **Have an accurate self-perception.** This component requires students to have a realistic perspective on who they are; it is engendered through feedback and reflection.
- **Recognize strengths.** Each student is unique in terms of both strengths and weaknesses. Realizing what those are, as well as building on strengths and dealing with or working on weaknesses, is important to students' sense of self.
- **Possess self-confidence.** When students are able to recognize and utilize their strengths, their self-confidence grows. Having self-confidence is vital to a strong sense of who they are.
- **Demonstrate self-efficacy.** Self-efficacy is students' belief in their ability to achieve a goal. Doing so requires a growth mindset.

This chapter provides many practices that you can use every day to help students become more self-aware about their emotions.

Self-Awareness in the Brain

Neuroscientists believe that the following brain regions are critical for self-awareness: the *anterior cingulate,* the *posterior cingulate,* the *medial prefrontal cortex,* the *insula,* and the *orbital prefrontal cortex* (see Figure 3.1). One of the reasons they know this is that in individuals with a history of chronic stress and trauma, these areas show very low activity. Van der Kolk (2014) found nontraumatized brains were actively engaging what he calls the "Mohawk of Self-Awareness" (shown as the dashed arrow in Figure 3.1). Here is how he describes these areas:

> [T]he midline structures of the brain [start] out right above our eyes [and run] through the center of the brain all the way to the back. All these midline structures are involved in our sense of self. The largest bright region at the back of the brain is the posterior cingulate, which gives us a physical sense of where we are—our internal GPS. It is strongly connected to the medial prefrontal cortex (MPFC), the watchtower.... It is also connected with the brain areas that register sensations coming from the rest of the body: the insula, which relays messages from the viscera to the emotional centers; the parietal lobes, which integrate sensory information; and the anterior cingulate, which coordinates emotions and thinking. (pp. 92–93)

Figure 3.1
Self-Awareness in the Brain

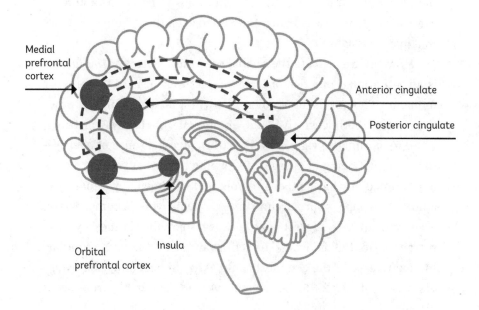

Medial prefrontal cortex

Anterior cingulate

Posterior cingulate

Orbital prefrontal cortex

Insula

Self-awareness is the only way we can access the emotional brain on a conscious level. The medial prefrontal cortex is the part of the brain that pays attention to what is going on inside us. For example, if we become angry, our amygdala, the small primitive emotional structure in the brain, can cause us to have an "emotional hijacking." At this point, we are using a reactive area in the brain that causes the release of the stress hormone cortisol, which surges through our body and may prevent logical thought. This action leads to the fight-or-flight response, which could cause us to do something we might regret. If we know that we are angry—that is, can name our emotion—our thought processes shift from the irrational amygdala to the thoughtful prefrontal cortex. It is there that we can make a choice as to what our response is going to be. Anger, sadness, fear, and other emotions are mediated by the limbic brain, and until we are aware of our feelings, the frontal lobe cannot assist in control. We need the frontal lobe structures to regulate our emotions. Furthermore, we know that the prefrontal cortex is not fully developed until the mid-20s—another reason why guidance is needed during the developmental years. Adults sometimes must act as a kind of external prefrontal cortex for students to keep them from behaviors that may be risky.

How can we activate the medial prefrontal cortex? *Mindfulness* is an intentional practice of focusing on awareness in the present moment. Thousands of studies confirm that mindfulness practices affect both cognitive and emotional function (Armstrong, 2019). According to van der Kolk (2014), giving a sense of *agency*— the feeling of being in charge, of knowing that what you say makes a difference in what happens to you, and of knowing you have the ability to shape your circumstances—helps you become aware. Some researchers suggest that because dopamine is the key neurotransmitter that activates the self-awareness structures, stimulating the release of the chemical could assist in becoming self-aware (Joensson et al., 2015). At school, we can aid in the release of dopamine by getting students up and moving and by engaging them in projects and working on goals (Panskepp & Biven, 2012).

Strategies for Teaching Self-Awareness

Although it may sound counterintuitive to teach someone how they feel, our purpose is to help students become aware of their feelings. We have all had the experience of feeling sad without knowing what led to that sadness. Some unrecognized trigger could have caused the sadness, such as driving by the cemetery where a loved one is buried. Or perhaps the sadness was building up over time, and because we didn't know how to deal with the emotion, it reached a point where it "bubbled over" and tears started to fall without our knowing why. The strategies in this chapter are to help our students become aware of what they are feeling, name the feeling, and have ways to deal with the emotion.

An Emotion Vocabulary

It has been proposed that we have basic emotions hardwired in our brains (Panskepp & Biven, 2012; Plutchik, 1997). Lisa Feldman Barrett (2018), a professor of psychology at Northeastern University, insists that emotions are *made*. Barrett says that we all have the same brain networks, but the wiring of those networks is dependent on our experiences. Therefore, we can infer that some of our students come to us with strong networks related to anger, for example, whereas others come with strong networks related to joy. Some students come to us with strong fear responses to circumstances that wouldn't bother most other students.

To begin to understand their emotions, students need words to express those emotions, words they can use to explain what they are feeling to themselves and to others. An emotion word wall is helpful for social-emotional learning (see Figure 3.2 for an example). You can help students increase their vocabularies by using the wall for writing assignments, as they elaborate on feelings experienced by characters in language arts, by real-world figures (historical or contemporary) in social studies, and by inventors and scientists in science classes.

Figure 3.2
Example of an Emotion Word Wall

Fear	Joy	Sadness	Anger	Disgust
afraid	blissful	anguished	annoyed	appalled
alarmed	calm	dejected	appalled	fed up
alert	cheerful	depressed	cold	nauseated
anxious	content	despondent	crabby	outraged
apprehensive	delighted	down	cranky	repelled
aversive	ecstatic	downcast	critical	repulsed
cautious	elated	drained	cross	revolted
distressed	encouraged	gloomy	detached	shocked
distrustful	enthralled	heartbroken	displeased	sickened
fearful	excited	melancholy	exasperated	
hesitant	friendly	miserable	frustrated	
horrified	happy	mournful	furious	
hypervigilant	hopeful	pessimistic	horrified	
jumpy	joyful	unhappy	hostile	
nervous	jubilant	weepy	injured	
paralyzed	lively		irked	
petrified	peaceful		irritated	
shaky	satisfied		livid	
shocked	smiling		mad	
worried	thrilled		offended	
			ranting	
			resentful	
			riled up	
			seething	
			slighted	
			vengeful	

Often students use basic "feeling" words, such as *happy, sad, mad, confused,* and *scared*. Providing a variety of vocabulary words related to emotion may help in expressing a feeling more precisely. The more words we have to describe how we feel, the better we will be able to know ourselves and relate to others. If we can label an emotion, we can begin to figure out what to do about it. And labeling can lower the activation of the amygdala while raising the activation of the prefrontal cortex, which helps with regulation of emotions (Brackett, 2019).

Greetings

Chapter 1 included greetings as a strategy for building relationships with students, and here are a few other ideas for greetings that pertain to self-awareness. Greetings offer an opportunity not only to develop relationships but also to discover how your students are feeling. When walking into a home or a restaurant, someone is usually there to greet you, to make you feel at home. For many of our students, however, there is no one at home to greet them, talk to them, or answer questions. Students from households affected by poverty, divorce, trauma, or other negative situations may need a place to feel like home—and school may be their best "home." A greeting as they enter school or your classroom can be the initial contact that offers a feeling of belonging.

We speak of self-awareness as recognizing and understanding how we feel. Knowing someone is "seeing" and "hearing" them tells students that they are valued and have worth. This awareness helps in understanding and shining a light on how the students feel. Some of our students have been disconnected from their feelings owing to trauma. This disconnection comes from a survival mechanism in their brains that can disconnect them not only from their feelings but also from their bodily sensations.

You can make students feel welcomed and recognized in at least two essential ways: with a full-school greeting ("all hands on deck") and by offering individual greetings at the door at the beginning of the day (for self-contained classrooms) or at the beginning of each class period (for departmentalized classrooms).

Borrowing the navy phrase "all hands on deck" indicates that every adult in the building—from the principal to the custodians, the cafeteria staff, the teachers, the librarians, and others—is available to greet the students. If school is a home, then everyone should be happy to greet one another with a smile, indicating excitement about being there and anticipation of a good day.

Greeting students by name and including a positive statement at the beginning of class increased engagement by 27 percent, according to one study (Allday, Bush, Ticknor, & Walker, 2011). Simply greeting students at the door has been proven to increase student attention to learning, or on-task behavior (Allday & Pakurar, 2007), and it establishes teacher rapport with students.

A cautionary note for the start of the school year is to avoid using an opening statement as a way to check on homework or other academic matters. It may be tempting to say something like "Did you love the story we read last night?" or "I can't wait to see your project and hear how you feel about it!" or "I'm so excited to share today's lesson; you're going to love it!" This type of chatter is suitable only after a few weeks, when you have a good sense of students' personalities and abilities. You don't want to scare students and create stress if they haven't read the story or worked on their project. In fact, this can be the time to calm some nerves by saying, "If you didn't get to finish last night's story, I have a great way for you to help each other summarize it. No worries!"

An Emotional Inventory: Check-Ins

You may not have the time or the privacy to elicit personal feelings from your students at the door. A check-in is a great way to find out how each student is feeling, and it helps them to become more aware of themselves.

If you are lucky enough to have the time for a morning meeting, you can check in with students then. Here are some examples of nonthreatening cues that students could respond to at a morning meeting:

- Say a phrase, using five or fewer words, that describes your day yesterday.
- Finish this sentence: "The best news I've had in the past week is _____."
- Finish this sentence: "When I was little, I thought I wanted to be _____."
- Name one skill you have that no one in this group knows about.
- Finish this sentence: "The next time we meet, we should _____."
- What is one thing that you would like to accomplish before _____?
- What is the main challenge you face in the first 10 minutes of your day?
- How would your next-door neighbor describe you, in two words?

As a time-saver—especially for those who don't have a schedule that allows for a morning gathering—you can have students do an independent check-in. Some strategies follow.

Just One Word. When students are engaged in daily activities such as working on an art project, a math problem, or a writing assignment, write a question on the board and ask them to fill in the blank with just one word. Here are some examples:

- How you are feeling right now?
- What do you do when times get tough?
- How do you feel right now about your life? (You can substitute *friends, family, relationships,* or *school;* you know your students, so use what would be appropriate for them and their circumstances.)

- How do you feel about our class? (If students are not turning in their papers, walk around and see what they have written.)

Inside Out. If you haven't seen *Inside Out,* you may think it's a movie for kids, but I think it's meant for adults. Much of the Oscar-winning animated film by Disney/Pixar takes place in the head of an 11-year-old girl named Riley. It features five key emotions (joy, sadness, anger, fear, and disgust) inside her brain, portrayed through five characters who help Riley navigate the ups and downs of her life. Teachers often show the movie at the beginning of the year to launch a discussion about the feelings we all have at times.

Teachers in elementary, middle, and high schools have used the characters and their distinct colors (yellow for joy, blue for sadness, red for anger, purple for fear, and green for disgust) to help students label their emotions. Some teachers tape a small representation of each emotion on a chart on students' desks and ask them to check the chart periodically to note their feelings. Other teachers display a large wall chart where students check and identify their feelings. Again, as with the emotion word wall, this chart can be incorporated into content as you discuss the feelings of literary characters, political leaders, historical figures, and others.

"Check In Before You Check Out" Exit Passes. Used by teacher Jill Fletcher (2019), these exit tickets ask students questions such as *How are you feeling? What's new with you? What do you want to share with me?* Using these passes, she discovered that some students were actually sad, bored, or upset when they seemed engaged and outwardly happy. After just a few weeks, she got to know her students really well—better than she had known prior students. Several students wrote to say that their favorite thing about class was that she checked in with them every day and they were able to tell her how they were feeling.

Attendance Charts. Teachers at several elementary and middle schools I have visited use an attendance chart. Many are magnetic, with an alphabetical list of student names. When they enter the classroom, the students take a magnet that has a check on it to indicate their presence. To make this an emotional check-in, some teachers have replaced the attendance magnets with emoji icons or magnets with the *Inside Out* characters on them, giving the teacher an indicator of what state each student is in and a composite indicator of the class.

This strategy is helpful if something has recently occurred in or out of school that affects many students. For instance, after a 6th grader died in a car accident, it took many days of sad or angry emojis before the student's classmates were truly ready to dig into content. Their teacher paid close attention to the deceased student's friends, and she requested conferences with parents that led to setting up counseling sessions for some students. Other situations, such as problems on the bus or playground before school, can affect students' ability to focus. Early awareness can lead to prompt resolution of any problem and provide the opportunity for students to work successfully throughout the rest of the day.

Some P.E. teachers tape squares or circles of colored paper to walls in the gym at a level that all students can reach. When students are running (or skipping or walking) laps, they slap the color that represents how they feel. What's important about this strategy is that students see that all teachers are interested in how they are feeling.

Assigned Seating. "Assigned seats communicate to students that they are supposed to be there and they have a place where they belong" (Souers & Hall, 2016, p. 103). Assigned seating provides instant knowledge of who is present and who is not. It gives students a place to go when they enter your room (a safe space for them). If you add the "team" practice discussed in Chapter 6, each student "belongs" to a group. If you look over your seating chart and see that someone is missing, be sure to say something to the class like "Cassie isn't here. Does anyone know if she is ill?" or "Is she feeling any better?" Your students will know that they have a place where they will be missed. Whether they are present or not, you care enough to check in on them.

Remote Check-Ins. At the time of this writing, schools have been grappling with the most unusual circumstances we have ever encountered with the COVID-19 pandemic. Stay-at-home orders have affected almost everyone in the world. As teachers attempt to teach their students remotely for perhaps the first time, their stress levels are affected. Students wonder how seriously they should take this new approach to learning. Some are devastated that they cannot leave their homes and go to school, which they consider their safest place. Many are spending most of their time in front of a screen, either for school or for recreation.

Amid this crisis, checking in takes on a new dimension. Even under these somewhat bizarre circumstances, it is necessary to let students know that you care about how they feel. The media has spotlighted various ways teachers have been connecting and checking in with students. Some drive by their students' homes with signs indicating that they miss them and are thinking about them. Often, they stop to say hello from a distance. Others are doing individual video calls once a week to let their students know they care and to ask how they are doing. During remote classroom sessions, teachers can chat individually with students to ask how they are doing. Whatever the situation, teachers must and do find avenues for check-ins.

Journaling

When journaling about feelings was suggested as a classroom activity, an 8th grade language arts teacher said, "I don't have time for my students to take out their journals and write about their feelings," and a sophomore algebra teacher said, "I can barely get through the curriculum. I don't have a spare minute for feelings."

What these teachers need to realize is that *there is no learning without feelings*. Once students can recognize their emotions, they can learn skills to change them, which enables a focus on learning. "When we educators fail to appreciate the importance of students' emotions, we fail to appreciate a critical force in students' learning. One could argue, in fact, that we fail to appreciate the very reason that students learn at all" (Immordino-Yang, 2016, p. 40).

In his book *The Power of the Adolescent Brain,* Thomas Armstrong (2016) suggests journals as a way to help adolescents develop a sense of self-awareness. He offers suggestions for tying the journal to curriculum. For instance, in English language arts, students could keep a journal that represents the life of a favorite character; in history, they could keep a journal from the viewpoint of someone living in the historical period being studied. For science, Armstrong suggests students keep a "scientist's journal" instead of a lab notebook. All these suggestions help personalize the learning.

If you need some prompts for students' journaling, you may want to try some of the ones listed previously for check-ins at morning meetings. You can also use your content for journaling, as Armstrong suggests, and ask students to add their personal feelings about what you are studying. For instance, ask them how they feel about a literary character's decision. In math, one teacher has her students journal about the usefulness—or lack thereof—of certain theorems.

A handwritten journal has more than a social-emotional effect; it also makes a cognitive difference. A study of note taking found that the act of writing by hand activates more brain areas than keyboarding; it also causes students to think more about their learning (Mueller & Oppenheimer, 2014).

Journaling can be a mnemonic device, much like the "blank page" strategy I discuss in *How to Teach So Students Remember* (Sprenger, 2018). If you provide a blank sheet of paper for students to write down everything they remember about what was just studied, they are much more likely to remember the content.

It works better than reviewing the information through reading or multiple-choice questions.

According to Steven Stosny in his blog post "The Good and the Bad of Journaling" (2013),

> Journaling can have a positive effect on behavior and well-being if it:
> - Makes you step back and evaluate your thoughts, emotions, and behavior.
> - Explores solutions.
> - Brings your emotions and motivations into alignment with your deepest values.
> - Converts negative energy into positive creativity and growth.
> - Lowers your emotional reactivity to others.
> - Increases tolerance of ambiguity, ambivalence, and unpredictability, which are part of normal living.
> - Helps you see other people's perspectives alongside your own.
> - Makes you feel more humane.
> - Helps you take a definite course of action. (para. 3)

If your students need some inspiration for journaling, share this quote from champion tennis player Serena Williams: "Writing down your feelings in a notebook or journal can help clear out negative thoughts and emotions that keep you feeling stuck" (www.writing athletes.com/whats-an-athletes-journal.html). Add to the impact of this celebrity idea by putting a poster of Serena Williams in the classroom, with the quote beneath it. Ask your students what their favorite celebrity says about emotions.

Drawing

Artwork—particularly self-portraits—can be an effective way to ascertain students' feelings about themselves, and an art activity can be done easily without taking up much class time. I've added an art component to assignments in grades K–12, and it works well. When

I give students a reading assignment (in any content area), I may ask them to draw a picture of themselves indicating how they felt about the assignment. (Sometimes they only produce a stick figure, but that's OK.) I often put them in groups to discuss why they feel this way about the reading. The activity is quite revealing—and I'm teaching social-emotional intelligence along with my content. It's a starting point for them to think about themselves and their feelings about something that's not too personal. Later, I can ask them to show me how they feel about a topic or lesson using their own facial expressions. If I see a lot of confused faces, I know I have more explaining to do!

Having students draw pictures related to the content, rather than their personal reactions, often reveals feelings as well. As noted earlier, emotions are part of learning, and most kids like to draw, so it's a win-win. Offering students the option to "show what they know" through drawing—along with other means such as writing, acting, dancing, and music—allows them to express their feelings about the content and the impact it has on them.

Taking a Break

Most of us, adults and children alike, occasionally have to stop whatever we are doing to identify what we are feeling. I often find myself living my life and suddenly realizing that I am overwhelmed or upset, but I don't know why. I have to stop and "feel the feeling" for a few minutes before I realize that I'm sad, angry, or frustrated about something. The next step is to identify the cause of the feeling and deal with it. On the positive end of the emotional spectrum, I could be feeling joy and not giving my body and mind the opportunity to enjoy it.

Whether you call it a "brain break," a "feeling break," or just a "break," you can use this strategy with individual students, a small group, or the whole class, as necessary. If you notice students in a state that you are concerned about, ask them to take a break, and after a few minutes, check in with them to see if you can help. Some teachers call this a Stop, Feel, Solve (SFS) break.

"I Wish My Teacher Knew..."

The more we know about our students, the better able we are to meet their needs in the classroom. Third grade teacher Kyle Schwartz (2016) found this out in a simple way. She asked her students to complete this sentence: "I wish my teacher knew _____." She discovered more than she expected. Among the responses were these: "I wish my teacher knew that we live in a shelter"; "I wish my teacher knew that my dad died this year; I feel alone and disconnected from my peers"; "I wish my teacher knew that my mom might get diagnosed with cancer this week." There were positive wishes as well, such as "I wish my teacher knew that I learn better when I'm listening to music" and "I wish my teacher knew that I love my family." These revelations remind us to be aware of how students' "wishes" can affect learning.

Self-Perception "Boots"

Through feedback and reflection, students can consider closely who they are and who they want to be. Just as reflecting on how they learn best can lead to becoming a better learner, reflecting on how they feel and think—metacognition—can help them become better at determining how they want to live and what will lead to a better life.

In *Fostering Resilient Learners* (Souers & Hall, 2016), Kristin Souers uses a metaphor of cement shoes to visualize what our sense of self does for us. She tells us that if we were in the ocean and waves were coming at us, without something to keep us grounded (like cement shoes), we would soon lose our balance. Our cement shoes are our beliefs about ourselves, our ideals and integrity.

Using this metaphor, or another of their choosing, ask students to draw a pair of boots (which are larger than shoes and give them more room) and write on the boots what the cement is that keeps them grounded. You could alternatively have them write a paragraph or a short story about their boots.

Listening to the Body

Our feelings are closely associated with what is going on inside our bodies. With some students, it is helpful to ask them to "listen" to what their body is telling them. Is their heart beating quickly? Are their palms sweaty? Do they feel a need to move around? Knowing *what* we feel is the first step in knowing *why* we feel that way.

Because many of our students have been told that what they are feeling (or doing) is wrong, they have learned to suppress their feelings. As a result of this suppression, these students don't trust themselves. For them, the gut feelings that we all get or the predictions that we make become just another sign to hide. In fact, those students' feelings are warning signs from their bodies, and the more they try to push them away, the more they take over (van der Kolk, 2014).

Until students have a good relationship with their bodies, they are unable to go to the next step of self-regulation. *Alexithymia* is the Greek word for not having words for feelings. People with alexithymia tend to look at emotions as physical problems. Instead of knowing how they feel, they may try to get away from those feelings. Students may be disconnected from their feelings related to traumatic events or misguidance from their caregivers. They simply can't describe what they are feeling because they cannot connect feelings with the physical sensations in their bodies. Instead of anger or sadness, they have stomachaches, muscle pain, or another ailment.

One of my students who came from a middle-class home with two parents and several siblings could not connect with her feelings because she was taught not to show emotion, as it might cast a shadow on the family. When they were small, she and her siblings were told never to cry, and if they started to do so, they were threatened. As just one example, she told a story of herself, at the age of about 5, in the doctor's office with her mother. She started to cry when the nurse told her she would need a vaccination for school. Her mother looked at her with disdain and said, "Don't you cry. If you cry, I am going to leave you here." Her mother's words were frightening, and the girl withheld the tears.

Identifying Strengths and Weaknesses

Students who can identify their strengths will be able to build on them. Their self-confidence will increase as they are motivated to work harder in these areas. As you build relationships with your students, you can use the 2 × 10 strategy described in Chapter 1 to help them (e.g., "Did you see the game on Friday night? Would you like to pitch against the Blue team?").

Research on the brain and learning shows us that there are steps we go through as we learn skills and concepts (Sprenger, 2018). You could ask your students to write a journal entry about what they are good at and how they became good—what steps were involved. The same strategy could help them address weaknesses and how they feel they could improve. What steps would they take? What steps are missing that were included in their earlier entry about strengths?

"Personal branding" is an activity that some businesses and individuals undertake when they want to create a sense of who they are and what they stand for. Students can think of brands of products they like and use social media, research sites, and interviews with other students to define the strengths of the product. Then you can ask them to come up with a personal brand. To help them do so, you can have them answer some simple questions via journaling: *Who inspires me? What is it about them that is inspirational? What am I good at? What am I—or could I be—great at?*

They might create an infomercial or a social media post that paints the picture they want others to see of them. Tracy Brighten (2017) suggests that we help students write blogs and create websites to showcase their strengths, talents, and interests. Through social media, they can connect with other students who have the same interests or with experts in the areas in which they have talents.

Self-Confidence Builders

Keeping in mind the previously discussed components of self-awareness (understandings of feelings, strengths, and values), a natural next step is to help students develop their self-confidence. Four factors can guide the process:

- **Praise.** When appropriate, praise students both personally and publicly. Positive statements will help them feel good about their accomplishments, and if need be, you can follow (privately) with observations about something they need to work on.
- **Choice.** Students feel good about themselves and have a feeling of agency when they are allowed to choose and to voice their needs or desires about projects, content, and products.
- **Opportunity.** Give students the opportunity to share their strengths. You can begin by asking them about something you know they are good at, and you can ask them to help you or others in the same area.
- **Feedback.** Always provide feedback that students can build upon soon. Brookhart (2017) calls this a "feed forward" loop and says that feedback fails if it is not used in future learning.

Developing Self-Efficacy

Self-efficacy is the belief that you can succeed. It is also the knowledge that you have the power to change so you can reach the goals that you have set for yourself. Under this competency, I suggest two areas of focus: (1) teaching your students about the brain and (2) helping them to develop a growth mindset.

Why teach students about their brains? When your students understand why something is true, they are more likely to remember it and believe it. Specifically, when they understand how their brain works and how it can change, they will believe that they can have an impact on how successful they are in the classroom. First, they must understand that their brain changes as they make new connections and reinforce prior knowledge. When they are in class, I tell them that I am a brain-changer who offers opportunities for growth—and so are they. When they learn something new, their brain is changing. It changes by creating a new pathway, connecting existing pathways, and then strengthening those pathways as they revisit, repeat, and reflect on their learning. If they only play video games, their brains are changing in areas related to that activity and perhaps losing the strength of connections in other areas. Students can learn that they, indeed, are the "boss" of their brain.

What is a growth mindset and why is it important? Students with a supposed "fixed mindset" toward learning believe that the ability to do well in school is something that they were born with. But Carol Dweck (2016) believes that everyone can learn if they work hard, and that those who hold this belief will do better at school than those with fixed mindsets.

Teaching your students that their brains are like muscles can be a great metaphor for understanding the idea behind the concept of a growth mindset. If you go to the gym and work out, your muscles get stronger. The same is true of your brain: the more you work at learning and problem solving, the easier those things become.

Stories to foster a growth mindset are available for all ages. *Amazing Grace*, by Mary Hoffman, is a book I've used for this purpose with my middle school students.

Students sometimes set goals for improvement without reflecting on how their strengths can help them achieve those goals, so they become frustrated and want to give up. When working with students, focus on their strengths as the tools for improvement. And don't forget the power of *yet:* "You're not there *yet.* You'll get there!"

A short questionnaire may help students home in on their mindset. Here are some sample questions:

- Do you give up easily? Could you change so that you give up less easily?
- When you are faced with a difficult task, how likely are you to stick with it?
- How confident are you that you can find ways to accomplish your goals?

The concept of a growth mindset can apply to students' understanding of emotions. Once they can recognize emotions, they can grow in the ability to describe emotions and their causes, identify factors that create emotion, analyze how emotions affect behavior, and evaluate how emotions affect others.

Every Student Has a Story

"Self-awareness has meaningful consequences that can impact your relationships and your day-to-day well-being," says Robin Stern of the Yale Center for Emotional Intelligence (Graves, 2017, p. 10). Being unable to label your feelings is frustrating. We must keep in mind that every student will have a different level of emotional self-awareness. As we try to help students become more self-aware, what we say in response to their statements is important. Being more empathic with our responses will help our students accept and recognize their emotions. The following are some relevant if/then statements.

If a student says…	Say this…
"I can't do it."	"You can't do it *yet!* We'll work on this together."
"I didn't do this very well."	"What do you think you could have done better?"
"This is too hard."	"Who do you think could help you with this?"
"I have nothing to do."	"What are your two favorite things to do?"
"I can't do math. My mom couldn't do math either."	"Remember how your brain changes when you learn? You can train your brain to do math. How would you like to begin?"
"I don't feel well."	"Is your stomach [or head, etc.] really bothering you, or could it be something else?"
"Fine," in response to your asking "How are you?"	"Really, how are you?"
"I feel sad, but I don't know why."	• "Are you thinking about something that makes you sad?" • "Would you like to talk to the counselor?" • "Why don't you go to the calming spot [or the reading spot, etc.] and think about it for a while? It can take some time to figure out why we feel the way we do."

4

Self-Management

If you want her to do well in math in her later years, the greatest thing you can do is to teach her impulse control in her early years.

—John Medina

When the students walk into the classroom, I have a letter in my hand. I explain that this letter, which appears to have been written after a bad breakup, was left in the printer. I don't want to betray anyone's trust, but I think we need to find out who wrote this. I begin to read the following:

Dear S. M.,

Life isn't the same without you. I am finding that as the year passes, I need you more and more. I cannot get anything accomplished without you. I am anxious all the time, I can't get organized or motivated, and I can't reach my goals.

I am constantly overreacting to other people's comments. I've been asked to leave classes, and I had to leave Melanie's party, too. I know if we were together—if you were a solid presence in my life—this would not happen.

Why did you leave me? Or did I never really have you to begin with? I think my brain has been flooded with stress hormones since you've been gone.

I never realized how important you are to me. What can I do to get you into my life? Will it help if I get down on my knees and beg? If you return to me, I promise to do better. To be better. I know I am groveling, but my heart is broken.

Hoping you can be mine again,

Me

The reveal: After students try to guess who wrote the letter and who S. M. is (Scott Matthews? Sabrina Myers?), I explain that the letter could have been written by any one of us. S. M. stands for Self-Management. I reread the letter for students to consider the context, then ask students if they can make any personal connections to the needs and losses indicated in the letter.

Self-management is about regulation. Emotions aren't just regulated, they are *coregulated*. It is through our relationships that we learn to regulate. So many of our students come into the classroom having experienced trauma and stress; they walk in *dysregulated*—unable to control or regulate their responses to certain stimuli. If we have been successful in helping them become aware of their emotions, we now need to provide them with strategies to help deal with those emotions—to exercise self-management.

CASEL (2017) identifies six components of self-management:

- Impulse control
- Stress management
- Self-discipline
- Self-motivation
- Goal setting
- Organizational skills

These components of self-management are interrelated in many ways. For example, impulse control affects self-discipline, and goal setting requires self-motivation and organizational skills. For students, the ability to regulate thoughts, emotions, and actions in various settings—such as during class, at lunch, before and after school, on the bus, and in the hundreds of places and situations kids get into—is at the core of self-management.

Self-Management in the Brain

Various structures and neurochemicals in the brain are involved in the interrelated components of self-management. For example, working toward goals (which includes using organizational skills) releases dopamine, the "feel-good" chemical, in the brain. Reaching goals provides the brain with much-needed serotonin, a calming chemical. Dopamine levels go down when a goal is reached, but if we are acknowledged for reaching the goal, the dopamine is replaced by serotonin. The serotonin, in turn, makes it easier to handle stress and control impulses. Do you see how this cycle works?

On the negative side, anger can cause the amygdala, the small primitive emotional structure in the brain, to launch an emotional "hijacking." Trouble can occur any time the emotional center of the brain pushes aside the thought processes based in the prefrontal cortex. At this point, a reactive area in the brain causes the release of the stress hormone, cortisol, which surges through the body and prevents logical thought. Cortisol also impedes the hippocampus, the structure right next to the amygdala that is a key player in memory formation. This situation can trigger a fight-or-flight response and an action we might later regret. If we *know* that we are angry—that is, we can name our emotion—our thoughts shift from the irrational amygdala to the thoughtful prefrontal cortex. (We can't name the emotion in the automatic area of the brain, which is reflexive; we name it in the frontal lobe, where the speech center is located.) The ability to reach that frontal lobe when we are dealing with intense emotions and then to name those emotions is at the heart of self-management. It is there—in the prefrontal cortex—that we can choose what our response is going to be (see Figure 4.1).

Figure 4.1
Self-Management in the Brain

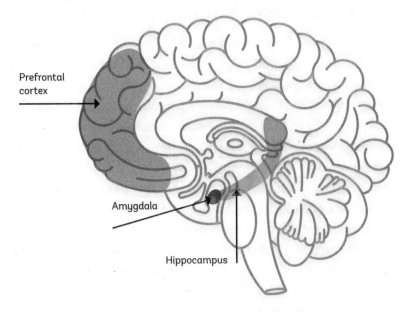

Strategies for Teaching Impulse Control

Pamela Cantor (2019) of Turnaround Schools explains that children's ability to have self-control is directly related to the context in which they are asked to have that control. If they are in a context with an adult they trust, they are more likely to control their impulses.

You may be familiar with the famous "marshmallow test" of the 1960s, in which researchers at Stanford University did a study of 4-year-old preschoolers (Shoda, Mischel, & Peake, 1990). These children were each offered a marshmallow and told that the experimenter had to leave the room. If they waited to eat the marshmallow until the experimenter returned, they would receive two marshmallows. Waiting was an impossible challenge for some of the children, but some did wait a seemingly very long time and managed to get the second treat. It so happened that this group of preschoolers—those who refrained from eating the marshmallow in order to receive another—grew up to be more successful and had higher scores on their SATs.

A similar study done in 2012 at the University of Rochester (Kidd, Palmeri, & Aslin, 2013) provided a little more information. Twenty-eight preschoolers were divided into two groups, one called the "reliable" group and the other the "unreliable" group. Children in the unreliable group were first asked to do a project that required coloring. The crayons they were offered were used and broken. The researcher told them if they could wait a few minutes, they would get some new crayons to use. In just a few minutes, the researcher returned and apologized, for there were no better crayons for them and they would need to use the broken ones. Next, the children were given a small sticker and told that if they waited a few minutes, they could choose from bigger and better stickers. Again, the researcher returned and apologized because there were no big stickers. The reliable group had the same setup, but their researcher always returned with the promised items. When offered one marshmallow with the promise of another if they waited for the researcher to return, the children who had received what they were promised waited much longer than the children in the unreliable group.

The message of this story is that trust matters. Experience matters. It is easier to delay gratification and control impulses if the context surrounding the experience is one of protection, trust, and an adult who follows through (Kidd et al., 2013).

Impulse control and self-discipline (which is discussed in detail later in this chapter) go hand in hand. They include the ability to recognize triggers and either avoid them or change the automatic behavior that would normally be exhibited. In essence, we are creating new pathways in the brain to replace inappropriate responses with appropriate responses. This reality shows us how important it is to first recognize emotions so that they can be controlled.

Another important component of impulse control (and self-discipline) is the ability to be a good listener. Good listening leads to better understanding of what is being said as well as the manner and tone of the person delivering the content. More favorable reactions occur when there is clarity about the situation.

What are typical school situations that show poor impulse control? Among the many are speaking out, interrupting classmates, quitting games, shoving in lines, cutting in front of others, jumping up from seats, asking questions about irrelevant topics, and displaying physical impulses and hyperactive behavior. You could probably add to this list.

Teachers often teach impulse control and delay of gratification with statements such as these: "We can't line up yet; the desks are not cleared"; "If we wait five minutes to leave for lunch, the lines in the cafeteria will be shorter"; "You may have an extra 10 minutes to work on your project if you keep the noise level a little lower." Such statements are helpful; however, it's getting to the root of the problem that will make the difference.

Breathing Exercises

Elias and Tobias (2018) suggest that students use breathing exercises to control their impulses. There are many online resources that can guide students through breathing techniques (see, for example, www.healthline.com/health/box-breathing#slowly-exhale).   The

"Mindfulness" section (pp. 101–103) offers more breathing exercises that can help students build this crucial skill.

The Feeling Thermometer

Using a feeling thermometer for impulse control works well at all grade levels. Older students (Elias & Tobias, 2018) can fill in individual feeling thermometers when something causes them to lose control; they can create this themselves, or you can distribute preprinted sheets. At the top of the sheet, have them write down the date and what they are feeling (e.g., anger, disappointment, or frustration). Below this is a three-column table. In the left-hand column, labeled "What Happened," students describe the event or circumstances that precipitated their feelings. In the right-hand column, labeled "Thoughts," students record their thoughts about the situation. These can be any thoughts running through their minds—for example, "I hate _____," "My parents don't care about me," or "Nobody likes me at school." Finally, students use a marker to fill in an image of a thermometer in the middle column to indicate how "hot" their feelings are. Run through the technique with the entire class, and remind students that in the heat of the moment, they may want to first try a breathing technique to calm down and keep themselves from saying something inappropriate before they have had the chance to reflect on the occurrence.

If you're an elementary teacher, you can hang a large feeling thermometer on the wall that indicates a temperature range from cool to hot. Students who are upset can go to the thermometer and put their name or initials next to the level of feelings they are having. For instance, a student who just experienced an upsetting incident on the playground may go up to the thermometer and write their name next to a "very hot" temperature. You can use this as a check-in strategy and find out what happened in a private conversation with the student. You could even put laminated thermometers on each student's desk so that students can mark how they are feeling throughout the day.

Strategies for Teaching Stress Management

Understanding what stress is and how your brain responds to it is essential in grasping the enormous effect it has in our lives and the lives of our students. Nadine Burke Harris, founder of the Center for Youth Wellness in San Francisco and surgeon general of the state of California, interprets the science in a way that all can understand in her book *The Deepest Well* (2018).

Burke Harris explains that what we face in our classrooms every day are students who have dysregulated stress-response systems. Some students experience stress and trauma and do *not* have dysregulation; just as our brains are unique, our ability to respond to stressful situations is also unique. One of the key criteria for dealing effectively with adversity or common daily stressors is having someone we can connect with. (It always goes back to relationships!)

You may have heard the expression "Sometimes you eat the bear, and sometimes the bear eats you!" Burke Harris uses a bear metaphor to explain the stress response. Sometimes we find the bear in the woods, but often we find the bear at home, and the response in the brain and body is the same. We know that some students are living with hunger, abusive caregivers (or no caregiver), parents in prison, physical or sexual abuse, or numerous other scary, untenable situations. Burke Harris studied children from low-income areas, but as we know, there are bears in the lives of students from high-socioeconomic-status households as well, and in urban, suburban, or rural settings. The stressors may be different, but nonetheless, what is going on in the brains of our overstressed kids is much the same.

When you face the bear, the amygdala reacts and the chemicals start flowing. Adrenaline and noradrenaline get your body amped up, but at the same time, so much is flowing that the focus of the prefrontal cortex is dimmed. This means there is no thinking straight, no way to stop the amygdala response. According to Burke Harris, the fear center shuts down the thinking brain so you can do the impossible. You can fight the bear—or run, or freeze. Digestion stops when this situation happens because, as Robert Sapolsky (2017) says in his book *Behave*, "[I]f you're running for your life, avoiding being someone's lunch, don't waste energy digesting breakfast" (p. 27). When we read a story about a mother lifting a car off her child to save the child's life, we're reading about the stress response that prevents the mother from knowing that she can't possibly lift the car. Nevertheless, she does. I like telling my students that story because I want them to believe that they can beat the odds, too. Fight the bear! Lift the car! Superhuman feats are possible.

Here's the issue: the stress response is supposed to level off and bring you back to your regulated state. As your body wants to get you back in balance (homeostasis), it will attempt to change the situation. A little stress with a period of rest for the brain and the body is ideal. But if you are facing bears every day—and sometimes dozens of times per day—the response can become *dysregulated*. The stress thermostat is broken as a result of repeated and intense use. And so we have students who are always hypervigilant, waiting for the bear. We have students who have shut down their feelings as a defense against the bear. We also have students who have daily stressors as a result of their social status at school. We have them all.

Some of our students are dealing with adverse childhood experiences, or ACEs, as I mentioned in the introduction to this book. These include stressful or traumatic childhood events such as abuse, parental imprisonment, divorce or separation, substance abuse, and death. We can help, and it begins with educating ourselves on stress and stress management. We need to understand that when trauma and stress go unchecked, they can impede and change brain development and affect memory, recall, focus, and impulse control

(Gaines, 2019). As previously noted, we can use SEL to help provide some positive childhood experiences to mitigate the effects of ACEs.

It is important to note that there are three kinds of stress. *Positive stress* occurs when students prepare for an athletic event or perhaps a presentation. This kind of stress is an important part of child development; the brain needs a bit of stress to allow it to adapt to the ups and downs of life. *Tolerable stress* is a more pronounced response to a difficult situation, such as the loss of a loved one. It's an event that is out of the student's control. It may last a while, but with help from the support that characterizes strong relationships, the body recovers. *Toxic stress* occurs when students face adversity without the help and support of an adult. Research (Center on the Developing Child, n.d.) suggests that students should face positive and tolerable stress to balance their stress response systems, but with some students, tolerable stress can slip right into toxic stress.

All I did was turn out the lights. The room was not completely dark, but it didn't matter. Margaret jumped up from her seat and ran out the door to the restroom across the hall. I thought she was ill. I asked her friend and classmate, Tamara, to check on her. "You better come, Mrs. S.," Tamara told me upon her return. I turned on the video I had been about to play when Margaret left, with strict instructions for students to remain in their seats.

In the restroom I found Margaret curled up in a corner of a stall, crying and shaking. I sat with her for a few minutes. She grabbed my hand and held on to it until she was ready to go back to class. I offered to take her to the office or the nurse, but she begged not to go. She didn't want her parents to be called. I respected her wishes to keep her calm, and we went back to the classroom. But that wasn't the end of it.

Margaret had occasionally come to school early and spent time just sitting in my room. I have always allowed students to do so, no questions asked. I was giving them a safe space in which they could talk to me or just sit. Margaret began coming in every morning and stayed after school as well. Eventually, she was able to open up to me about the long-term sexual abuse she was enduring, not from a family member but from a babysitter. We were able to get her the help she needed, and although she had been wary of telling her parents about the situation, as she thought it was all her fault, they came through for her.

The toxic stress from abuse that Margaret had endured for several years caused many reactions similar to the one described in the anecdote. Turning off the lights was only one trigger. With the help of a therapist, Margaret slowly improved.

It's important to acknowledge that as of this writing, the world is still reeling from the COVID-19 pandemic, which has exacerbated existing stress. As students begin returning to school, there are bound to be consequences from fears they may still hold and from the dysregulation of their nervous systems. When the brain lives in a state of fear and feels out of control, changes will have taken place. Relaxing those fears is the only way to get back the relationships you previously had with students, and to grow new relationships. Students will need a lot of predictability, including a schedule to follow and any other ways to let them know what is going to happen next. In the midst of the pandemic, no one knew what would happen. Entire countries of people lived in a state of fear. Learning does not take place when the brain is in this state; the brain can only try to survive. Your students' capabilities will be fluid and can change rapidly when cognitive, emotional, and social capabilities shift according to the brain state they are in. They will be coming to you from deep states of stress, and that kind of stress exhausts the body and brain. According to Dr. Bruce Perry (2020), we can expect our students to be less likely to focus and to be more irritable. We will need to move them from their state of fear and stress to a state of alertness and, eventually, calm.

So the question is, *How do we help students handle their stress?* If they can't handle their stressors, they won't be able to learn. Recognizing stress and managing it leads us to classroom strategies that can help.

Predictability: Routines, Structures, Rituals, and Procedures

According to Linda Darling-Hammond and colleagues (Darling-Hammond, Flook, Cook-Harvey, Barron, & Osher, 2019), the use of effective routines, structures, and procedures helps reduce stress and expedite learning for all students, including those who have experienced trauma or who struggle with behavior. Harry Wong and Rosemary Wong (2018) stress the use of procedures for classroom management. But the implication involves much more than that. Routines, rituals, and procedures help students feel safe and under control. Following a series of practiced and recognizable processes like routines and procedures allows the amygdala to be calm; there appears to be no danger in those processes. Consider the analogy of driving a car. With experience, the procedures for driving become automatic, and you almost mindlessly drive comfortably until something occurs that is outside the perceived routine. But if the driver in front of you suddenly slams on their brakes, you have to slam on yours to avoid a collision. If the traffic light quickly turns from green to yellow, you need to decide whether you have time to go through the light or if you must stop. If you hear a siren and see flashing lights behind you, you must figure out whether you are being stopped or you should slow down or stop so the emergency vehicle can get by.

Isn't it great to know what is going to happen? Consider this scenario. Jim wakes up in the morning, and Mom has breakfast waiting for him at 7:00 so he can leave the house and catch the bus at the corner at 7:30. He arrives at school at 7:45, with just enough time to get to his locker, put his lunch away, and grab his books for his first-hour class. Mr. Brown is always late for class because he is having his last cup of coffee in the hall while talking to the P.E. teacher. Mr. Brown enters the room after the bell rings, and Jim knows he can continue talking to his neighbor for another five minutes as Mr. Brown searches for the attendance sheet. This is a predictable situation that allows Jim to feel safe.

Life isn't always like that. I remember walking home from school with my friend Jamie. She became distressed every day as we approached her street and even somewhat panicky as we arrived at her house. Many days, she would beg me to come in with her. You see, Jamie's mother was an alcoholic, so Jamie never knew when she walked into the house whether she would be greeted with hugs and kisses or with screams and slaps. Jamie loved school because she felt safe there.

I learned about predictability when I spent a summer traveling and training with brain researcher and author Eric Jensen. From Eric, I discovered the usefulness of ritual in the classroom. Rituals are simple repetitive acts that become predictable. They are stimulus-response events. Whenever a particular situation occurs, a particular response will follow.

Classrooms need many rituals to provide a feeling of security, which may help destress the students. I tell my workshop participants that they should have 15 to 20 rituals in place by the end of the first week of school. If that number seems high, you may change your mind as I give you some examples.

This is what happens at the beginning of my class: as the students enter, the song "Be True to Your School" by the Beach Boys is playing. I am standing at the door, greeting my students with a smile and a "Good morning, _____!" When the tardy bell rings, I turn off the music. I turn to the students and say, "If you have 100 percent of your teammates seated and ready to go, raise your hand and say 'Yes!'" The students raise their hands, and when I see which teams do not have their hands up, I check to see who is absent. This is a quick and easy way to take attendance. Then I say, "Turn to the person next to you and say, 'Good morning, I'm happy you're here today!'" My next step is to go to the lunch menu and pretend that I'm selling lunch. "Harry Potter fans, there are no kippers or porridge today, but we have my favorite from the cafeteria: spaghetti with meatballs! Who's joining me?" To avoid "lunch shaming," you may want to devise a way for students to sign up for lunch instead of raising their hands. The sales pitch reminds students about lunch (*Oh, I forgot my lunch! I'd better sign up for school lunch.*) and makes the school lunch program more appealing.

That five-minute homeroom period included five rituals: (1) the music, (2) the greeting at the door, (3) taking attendance, (4) saying something to a teammate, and (5) selling lunch. To create rituals, you must first think of the classroom situations you might encounter. The rituals do not have to occur daily; they should simply be performed whenever a particular situation occurs. Here are some examples:

- Birthdays (I always play a silly tape of cats meowing the "Happy Birthday" song.)
- Opening of class (I play "We Are Family" by Sister Sledge.)
- Closing of class (How about playing "Happy Trails to You" or "What a Wonderful World"?)
- When a student is going to read their work aloud (I have an "author's hat" the student must wear.)
- When a visitor interrupts the class (I teach my students to stand up and applaud! We don't often get visitors!)
- Lunchtime (I say, "Turn to the person next to you and say, 'I'm hungry!'")
- On a test day (I play the song "Celebration" because we are celebrating our learning.)
- Class dismissal (I say, "Turn to the person next to you and say, 'I grew dendrites today!'" Then I stand at the door and give each student a high five as everyone exits.)

Think about rituals that will work for you and your students. You must be comfortable with your rituals so your students will be comfortable too.

Will rituals make your class boring? No. Predictability puts students at ease, which enables you to use novelty. It's true that if you do exactly the same thing in a very repetitive manner every day, both you and your students may get bored—and boredom can be stressful. So balance is important. Rituals make room for challenge, novelty, and a little craziness, which make the classroom experience fun. Can you change your rituals? Absolutely. Just keep in mind that it will take some time for your students to become accustomed to the new one, and be sure to warn them before you change. Be predictable!

The 90-Second Rule

The 90-second rule may be the most important rule you ever learn and teach to your students. The gist of it is this: if we are experiencing stress, we need 90 seconds for the brain and body to cleanse itself (Bolte Taylor, 2006). What happens in that minute and a half is critical. Stressors stay with us because we can't let go of the negative emotion. It consumes us. We rant to ourselves and to anyone who will listen. "Did you hear how that student spoke to me? I can't believe it! No student has ever said anything like that to me! Wait till I tell the principal. I'm going to make sure that kid never sees the light of day!" Filling those 90 seconds with positive strategies is a way to counteract the stress. I have given students a quick formula to help: CBS, or count, breathe, squeeze. Counting can calm the brain and help us focus on something other than the trigger. Breathing in a structured fashion helps slow the heart rate and combats some of the chemicals coursing through the body. The final step is squeezing something, such as a stress ball, a small stuffed animal (for younger students), or just the hands—whatever students are comfortable with.

Tone of Voice

In a statement on the video "Demonstrating Self-Regulation with Tone of Voice," Linda Darling-Hammond (2019) says, "Developing a calm, neutral, assertive voice is part of the teacher's own self-regulation, which allows them to help students to be self-regulated and to be secure in the knowledge that the teacher will be receptive to them, but also in control." When you use a calm yet assertive voice, your students will feel cared for.

Because of my personal background, it took me a long time to develop this kind of voice. I grew up in a family of six, and there was a lot of yelling. I thought a loud voice—almost a scream—was normal (really!). It wasn't until I had my first class of kindergartners that I realized my tone was affecting others, so I literally had to "tone things down." When I moved to middle school, I needed to raise my voice a little, so I found myself in front of a mirror, practicing a calming voice with some assertiveness thrown in. Many of my students were living under conditions in which their caregivers argued loudly or screamed at them, or there were so many people in the household that one had to yell to be heard. At school, they needed a calm, neutral voice in order to develop their own calm, neutral voice.

It takes practice to control your emotions and the knee-jerk reactions that may be triggered in some situations with students. If you have mastered your own self-awareness, you can work on recognizing your feelings and managing how you speak to students. A stressed student needs you to model calmness. Your body language and your voice will communicate how the student should respond. The website *PBISWorld.com* has a helpful guide on the why, when, and how of using a calm, neutral tone (www.pbisworld.com/tier-1/use-calm-neutral-tone/).

Therapy Dogs

The Alliance of Therapy Dogs (2017) tells us that dogs can help students and teachers by creating a sense of calm. Such dogs have been helpful with traumatized students and used in emergency situations, such as the aftermath of a school shooting.

Dogs are nonjudgmental. They love everyone equally and unconditionally—something that many of our students don't receive anywhere but school. Sometimes dogs are used in counselor's offices, and I have seen them roaming school hallways (attended, of course!), looking for situations that need some calm. Just as a classroom pet can have social-emotional benefits, therapy dogs can help students. Lower levels of stress and anxiety and even increased attendance have been reported, and studies show lower cortisol levels and higher oxytocin levels in students who interact with therapy dogs (Grove & Henderson, 2018). That means less stress, more trust!

A little while ago, I returned to the school where I had taught most recently. All the kids and parents were talking about Charley, their new therapy dog. She is a puppy and still learning what is expected of her, but she has already won the hearts of everyone in the building. She has been used to calm the teachers, to listen to children read, and to de-escalate tense situations. Charley spends most of her time in the counselor's office or the principal's office, but she is a comforting influence on the whole school.

Mindfulness

Mindfulness gives students the ability to be fully present and aware of their emotions and behavior at any given time. Awareness of the connection among emotions, thoughts, and bodily sensations enables students to better regulate their emotions. Once they know which self-regulation technique works best for them, they can apply it whenever they feel they are losing control.

Mindfulness has the added benefit of boosting the attention network in the brain's frontal parietal system. Research (Dunning et al., 2019) shows that as students become more mindful, they have more cognitive flexibility. Mindfulness increases the number of

brain cells in the frontal lobe and the hippocampus (areas important for learning and memory), and decreases the number of cells in
the amygdala, where the fight-or-flight response originates, resulting in less reactivity. To further explain, a decrease in the number of
cells in the amygdala means there are fewer connections between
the amygdala and the prefrontal cortex (where high-level thinking,
focus, and planning are centered); fewer connections means fewer
instances of the brain setting off alarms.

Many different breathing techniques can be taught as part of
instruction in mindfulness. Choose one you like, teach it to your students, and offer them variations. Here are some examples:

- **Basic:** Breathe in through the nose and out through the
  mouth, slowly.
- **4 × 4:** Inhale through the nose to a count of 4, hold for a count
  of 4, exhale to a count of 4, and hold again for a count of 4.
  Some teachers use laminated squares on students' desks (see
  Figure 4.2) to guide students through this technique.
- **Cotton ball breathing:** Ask students to sit so they have
  no eye contact with anyone in the room. Hand them each a
  cotton ball and have them place it in the palm of their hand.
  Have each student breathe in and out slowly for one minute,
  controlling the cotton ball so that it moves from the palm to
  the fingertips. Ask them to notice how their breathing slows
  as they control the cotton ball. After a minute, have them slow
  down their breathing even more so that the cotton ball goes
  no farther than the point at which their palm and fingers meet
  (Tantillo Philibert, 2016).
- **Pinwheel breathing:** Give students pinwheels and have them
  concentrate on their breathing as they learn to control how
  fast the wheels spin. Although kids like to get the pinwheels to
  go as fast as possible, help them become aware of how slowly
  the pinwheels can spin with calm, slow breathing.

It is important to have students practice breathing techniques so that the techniques become an automatic response that they can use on their own to control their emotions and behavior. (However, before a test, you may want to lead students in a collective breathing exercise to calm any anxiety.)

Figure 4.2
4 × 4 Breathing

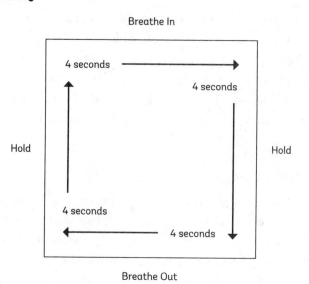

Calming Station

All grade levels can benefit from places in the classroom or building where students can calm their emotions. Known by various names—such as "calming station," "calming area," or "peace place"—this location might have a bean bag chair or some other comfy place to sit, or it might consist of a table and chair away from other students. It might include some stress balls or pinwheels to help with stress relief and regulation of breathing. The goal is to simply give students a place to regroup or refocus.

On a smaller scale, you might consider using a "calming bottle," which is simply a bottle filled with a combination of water, glue, and glitter. Students (and adults) like to shake the bottle and watch the glitter go from top to bottom, which takes a minute or two, so the 90-second rule is activated. If you don't think older kids will like this, just put one on your desk for a few days and see how many visitors you get. You can buy calming bottles or make your own ("recipes" are available at https://preschoolinspirations. com/6-ways-to-make-a-calm-down-jar/).

Frey, Fisher, and Smith (2019) share a strategy called TLC, used at their high school. It consists of a table and chairs in the hallway with a sign reading "How can I help?" A staff member sits at the table, and anyone can take a seat in the empty chair and engage in a dialogue or simply regroup.

Emotion Planner

The website *WeAreTeachers* (*WeAreTeachers*, 2018) suggests using an "emotion planner" for some students, and possibly for the entire class (see Figure 4.3 for an example). You can use the planner at the beginning of the day with your self-contained class or in your morning meeting. As a middle school teacher, I've used this idea during my brief homeroom period, and for high schoolers, I would use it at the beginning of first-hour class.

You can begin informally by asking your students how they are feeling, using simple questions like "What have you eaten this morning?" "Did anyone have an argument so far today?" "Were there any problems with your homework?" The answers will help you get a feel for what the day may be like for some students.

The planner shown in Figure 4.3 provides a more structured approach, with three columns labeled *Activity, Emotion,* and *Strategies*. If a test is on the schedule for a particular day, it may be helpful to write that under *Activity* and then discuss the possible emotions involved (your emotion word wall, described in Chapter 3, comes in handy here). Once you have listed emotions, let students offer strategies to handle those emotions.

Figure 4.3 **Emotion Planner**		
Activity	**Emotion**	**Strategies**
Science test	Anxious, nervous, stressed	• Take calming breaths. • Get a drink of water. • Review with a classmate.

Students can create personal planners, looking ahead at their day (or week) to anticipate when triggers for certain emotions may occur, and filling out the chart whenever they have time. You may want to check in with specific individuals who you know will benefit from a planner, adding this to the "check-in" tools you use (as discussed in Chapter 3).

Strategies for Teaching Self-Discipline

When we have lowered students' stress and taught them strategies for impulse control, we can move on to self-discipline. Response inhibition—the effortful control that becomes effortless control with practice—is what students do when they are able to choose a certain behavior over another, when we no longer have to discipline them because they do what they're supposed to do even when we're not watching! Here are some of the characteristics of a self-disciplined student:

- Asking for help when needed
- Staying on task
- Listening to directions
- Getting out materials when needed
- Coming to class prepared
- Turning in assignments on time

Party-Planning Experience

Developing a plan and then sticking to it is an important aspect of self-discipline. Whether you teach preschool or high school, planning ahead can be a challenge for many students. You can help them develop this skill by having them plan a party. What will they need? How much money will it cost? Who will the guests be? How will they let people know about the party?

After the party-planning experience, have students plan for a test or a project. Let them see how planning ahead helps them get things done.

Brain Break

Many students simply need a break. If the brain focuses for too long, it gets tired, which leads to mind wandering or daydreaming. Focused attention for most students is somewhere between 5 and 10 minutes. We may see students' need for movement at this point, too. If they don't get up and move around, they can easily disengage and miss the learning that is supposed to be taking place. Brain breaks offer a quick change in what the brain is doing. As students begin to lose focus, adding a little novelty changes the predictable routine. In its role as the brain's first gatekeeper, the reticular activating system determines what is coming into the brain. When things become too predictable and students lose focus, a brain interval wakes up the reticular activating system and allows students to begin to focus again.

A brain break can take various forms. Here are some examples:

- Movement that is content related ("Stand up and talk to three classmates about something related to the Civil War.")
- Movement for fun ("Walk around the room and don't sit down until you have touched three silver-colored objects and two gold-colored objects.")
- Singing or dancing
- Junk bag (Drawing from a bag filled with small household or office items, students pull out one item and come up with a new use for it.)
- Students walking around the room balancing a book on their head

Anything you can come up with to wake up the reticular activating system will work.

Strategies for Teaching Self-Motivation

Can they skip the concert and work on their project? Can they wait until they finish their homework to make a phone call to a friend? These are the types of questions whose answers tell us about our students' motivation—the drive to keep on task to achieve a goal.

Success Circle

Standing in front of a group of people to share a message almost always evokes a certain amount of stress and doubt. We ask ourselves, *Will I do a good job? Will my message be heard and understood? Will they like and appreciate my humor?* Some students feel the same way when they have to speak in front of a class to give a book report, share a project, or simply answer a question or contribute to the class dialogue. Situations such as these are when a "success circle" can help as a self-motivator. I tell my students to imagine a circle on the floor just a step away from them. This is the success circle. When they step into the circle, they can become a superhero, a person of great knowledge who can help others. Talk with them about literary characters, historical figures, or superheroes who stepped in to assist others. Before they "step in," have them take a deep breath and imagine themselves doing well. Then have them step into the circle, put their hands on their hips, and say to themselves, "I can do this! I *am* a superhero!"

Makerspaces

The emergence of "makerspaces," in which individuals with common interests share knowledge, tools, and resources in a common space, has had an impact on student learning that goes beyond cognition. Used as a vehicle for learning, makerspaces—which can be high- or low-tech—enable students to understand the value of self-motivation, self-discipline, and interdependence as they work with others on student-centered inquiry and creative projects. When students meet in these spaces, ideas are exchanged, support is offered, and failure *is* an option! Like collaboration, makerspaces help kids feel less isolated as they work to figure things out together. When students are isolated, failure can lead to giving up. But when students support and assist one another, they are more likely to move on from failure and try again.

Strategies for Teaching Goal Setting and Organizational Skills

Goals bring out the important characteristics of focus, perseverance, and grit. When students are willing to work toward a goal, despite setbacks, they show their ability to focus and persevere. As they encounter roadblocks or distractions and keep working toward the goal, they show their grit. The student who practices piano 30 minutes every day, the soccer player who runs each day to build up endurance, and the student who edits and rewrites papers, stories, and poems have all set goals for themselves and persevere even if it means missing a favorite TV show, not playing video games, or turning down an opportunity to go out with friends.

In the brain's prefrontal cortex, executive functions can develop through goal setting. The brain learns with maximum efficiency when it is motivated by goals that are both challenging and achievable. Brains are goal driven if they see the goal as relevant and having value (McTighe & Willis, 2019).

With these points in mind, you may find that some students will need guidance if given the opportunity to set their own goals. Often students write down goals that require more scaffolding to be achievable. You may have to help them break down long-term goals into a series of step-by-step, short-term goals. Students also need to be able to prioritize their goals.

Developing and prioritizing specific, measurable goals and a plan to achieve them requires organizational skills. Students can ask themselves questions such as the following:

- What is it that I want to achieve? (This should be clearly stated.)
- How will I achieve it? What steps will I take?
- What will "Plan B" look like if I run into obstacles?
- When will I achieve my goal? (It is important to put a time limit on the goal.)

- How will I know that I have reached my goal? (Depending on the content area, reaching the goal may be the completion of a project, a paper, or an assessment.)

I like to add the question "How will I celebrate my accomplishment?" The brain likes goal setting, which causes the release of dopamine, that "seeking chemical," in the prefrontal cortex.

Setting personal goals will help students understand the concept of delay of gratification. This concept can be taught at the earliest grade levels but needs reinforcement up through adolescence. Students can make visual representations of their goals through drawings or computer images, and they can write down (or represent in picture form) the steps to achieve the goal. Doing so will enable them to understand delay of gratification as they see where they are in the process of reaching the goal.

If your students sometimes work in teams, you may ask each team to develop goals related to their work together. Doing so can be good practice for students as they learn to develop personal goals. Team goals should be written down, but not necessarily posted publicly. Instead, students can write the goals in their notebooks so that both you and they can check progress.

Every Student Has a Story

As we work with students to help them control their impulses, manage their stress, and develop their self-discipline, self-motivation, and goal-setting and organizational skills, we want to provide positive experiences to help them cope and succeed. Anything we say or do can have a consequence. We don't need to know all the details of their stories, but we need to accept them for who they are; offer them safety, empathy, and a loving relationship; and try to make their lives better. Students who come to us with many adverse childhood experiences need help to find positive experiences in their lives. Consider the following if/then scenarios.

If...	Then...
Your class seems to be highly stressed,	Add more predictability in the form of procedures and rituals, and go over the 90-second rule with them.
You are dealing with many stressed and traumatized students,	Practice mindfulness, provide stress balls, and teach breathing exercises.
Students are not turning in work on time,	Discuss what is preventing them from doing the work and provide help with the content, if needed; talk about time management, if necessary; or provide extra time in a calm spot, if possible.
A student is not listening,	Review good listening practices and offer time or space to refocus.
A student is not staying focused,	Be sure you are providing brain breaks to give time to refocus.

If...	Then...
Individual students look stressed and have trouble functioning or participating,	Have them try the CBS (count, breathe, squeeze) strategy, or consider letting them go to a calming area in your classroom or building. We can't expect students to focus if they are fighting "bears" somewhere in their lives.
Students have done poorly on an exam or a project,	Remember that stress levels are up under these circumstances—there's more cortisol in their bodies and brains. It can take 24 hours for students to return to a state of homeostasis, or balance. Let them relax, talk to someone, or try breathing exercises. Remind them about the importance of a growth mindset (see Chapter 3).

5

Social Awareness

The brain is most interested in survival and has a deep need for relating to others.

—John Medina

Anika was the new girl at school. She had moved to the area right before the beginning of 7th grade. The girls in the neighborhood seemed to accept her right away, inviting Anika to walk to school with them and, more important, saving a spot for her at their lunch table. Anika had always been a little shy. She thought her name was awkward and hard for people to pronounce correctly, so she was timid when meeting new kids.

The Halloween dance was coming up, and Anika's mom bought her a great outfit that made her look like a Beatnik—red tights, white shorts, a white sweatshirt, and a red beret. Red was Anika's favorite color, and it suited her. From the way everyone looked at her when she entered the cafeteria, she knew she looked good!

Many of the boys asked her to dance, and, as was his custom, Mr. Wallace, the 8th grade teacher who ran and chaperoned the dances, also asked her to dance. He asked her how things were going for her at school. Was she making friends? Did she have any questions about the school or her classes? Feeling like the belle of the ball, Anika chattered away to Mr. Wallace. School was great, her friends were good, and she knew just what everyone was doing. Then she began to tell him about her friends and their secrets—or at least things they didn't want anyone outside their circle to know. Anika was not usually this chatty, but she couldn't seem to help herself, and she began to tell Mr. Wallace more than he should know. He tried to change the subject and lead her toward more appropriate conversation, but Anika was on a roll, and rambled on about who had crushes on whom, who was doing things behind her friend's back, and anything else she could think of to share. Although Mr. Wallace lowered his voice to try to get her to lower hers, nothing worked. In fact, Anika felt so powerful that when the dance ended, she went over to her new friends and told them what she had told the teacher. She had no clue how inappropriate she was being. And so her downfall began.

Social awareness is the ability to take the perspective of and empathize with others, including those from diverse backgrounds and cultures. It includes walking into a room and understanding the climate and the inner states of people, and knowing whether to speak and, if so, what to say and how to say it. Thus, this chapter focuses on empathy, perspective taking, and respect for others, all of which are important components of social awareness. All are skills that Anika lacked.

Reiterating the importance of empathy, I encourage you to use the strategies discussed in Chapter 2, including the importance of a complete "emotion vocabulary." The more fully we understand and can label emotions, the easier it is to recognize them and to understand and deal with others. Using your emotion word wall will help students gain this understanding. One quick strategy is to play an alphabet game in which students come up with as many emotion-related words as they can for each letter of the alphabet. Another is to say, for example, when students are lining up for lunch, "I need five emotion words for *angry!*" It's fine if they look at the word wall; we want them to get more comfortable using words like *upset, disappointed, annoyed, furious,* and *irate.* These words alone begin to tell a story.

It is our job as educators to help our students to recognize their own emotions and other people's emotions; to use information about emotions to guide thinking and behavior; to discern the thoughts, feelings, and motivations of others; to understand how others view a particular situation; to understand social and ethical norms for behavior; to recognize and use family, school, and community resources and supports; and to be aware of their own cultural identity and views about cultural differences. (Do you feel like you have to take a breath after reading that?)

All students continually attempt to make sense of their own and others' behaviors; doing so helps them guide their interactions with others. The inability to understand or interpret emotions can make school seem overwhelming. Students with strong social awareness adapt more easily to their environment, empathize with the perspectives of others, and engage in fewer disruptive classroom behaviors. They are able to engage in constructive communication with their peers and resolve conflicts when they arise.

Many students come to school with these abilities. In these cases, we can help them refine such areas as attunement—that is, listening with full receptiveness and connecting to people. Our students need to sense nonverbal emotional signals as well as understanding others' thoughts, feelings, and intentions. Finally, they need to know how the social world works and how to shape the outcomes of interactions.

Social Awareness in the Brain

The *inferior parietal lobe* is the area of the brain that encodes familiarity, social distance (the distance between groups based on such factors as class, race/ethnicity, and gender, among others), and perspective taking, whereas the *medial prefrontal cortex* encodes how socially relevant other people are to us. The *cerebellum* aids in the interpretation of socially relevant signals to understand intentions as well as the mental and emotional states of others. These signals may be verbal, or transmitted through *prosody* (elements of speech, such as intonation, pitch, and loudness, that provide clues about intended meaning), gaze, facial expressions, and movement (Sokolov, 2018). The *posterior superior temporal sulcus* (pSTS) is an area on the right side of the brain, behind the ear, that is involved in recognizing facial expressions (Srinivasan, Golomb, & Martinez, 2016). The *temporoparietal junction,* which is involved in thinking about others, and the *inferior frontal gyrus,* a region in the frontal lobe that supports thinking about abstract concepts such as belief and reality, are also involved. The connections among these structures become stronger as brains develop and kids have more experiences that enable them to empathize, pick up nonverbal cues, and realize that another person's intentions may not necessarily be in their own best interest—in other words, to understand the social interactions, large and small, that will happen every day of their life (Padmanaban, 2017). (See Figure 5.1.)

Researchers from the University of Oxford (Pearce et al., 2017) conducted a recent study showing that endorphins and dopamine play an important role in facilitating friendships and social networks. Endorphins help us relax and make us friendly and helpful, and dopamine is directly related to how well we connect with our friends.

In Chapter 3, which focused on self-awareness, we looked at ways to access the medial prefrontal cortex. Self-awareness and social awareness activate some of the same areas in the brain, which makes sense, because you must be aware of your own emotions to understand the emotions of others. In this chapter, we look at strategies to activate the areas of the brain for social awareness.

Keeping in mind that dopamine is a major player in social situations, offering students opportunities that lead to the release of dopamine is essential for social awareness. Panskepp and Biven (2012) have defined *play* as an emotion. Given that most people may question that definition, we can replace *play* with the term *social joy,* which is used by affective scientists (Gregory & Kaufeldt, 2015). Therefore, play, as an activity (which takes different forms at each developmental level), should be considered. Children and teens anticipate the fun in play, and that anticipation releases dopamine. When happiness is involved, endorphins are also released.

Figure 5.1
Social Awareness in the Brain

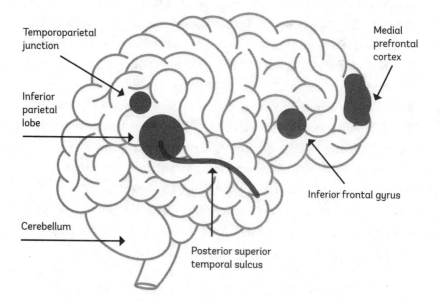

Prosocial Skills and Norms

The ability to understand and follow social norms is an important component of social awareness. Using *prosocial behavior* means taking positive actions that benefit others and are not prompted by personal gain. Prosocial skills are often guided by the norms that you have set up in your school and your classroom.

Setting up norms should be an endeavor in which all students participate. There may be distinctive norms for different content areas. In my English language arts (ELA) classes, we have norms for reading and norms for writing. Depending on the setup that day, we might add additional norms. I ask my classes, "What does learning in reading (or literature) look like and sound like?" In middle and high school, I have my students come up with adjectives that would describe us as we engage in these areas. (Notice the *us* and the *we;* the creation of norms is inclusive and gives students a feeling of belonging.) So for reading, the list may include words such as *focused, quiet, technology-free* (unless we are reading from tablets), *inclusive, calm, nonthreatening, active listening, collaborative,* and *enthusiastic.* When I ask, "What does group work look like and sound like?" the students determine which norms are most important for the task. *Focused* always makes the list, but *quiet* may not, as we are working together. For lower grades, the norms may include *be quiet, respect others, share, be prepared,* and *respect personal space.* I like the label "norms" better than "classroom rules" because norms aren't just what you're supposed to do; they describe the way you can *be!*

You or your school may certainly want to adopt other norms instead of, or in addition to, the ones I've mentioned here. The important point is to have some norms and use them to help your students be prosocial. Knowing what to do or how to behave beforehand gives kids an edge both in and out of school.

Social Pain: Is It Real?

Along with social awareness comes "social status awareness." Every classroom has hierarchies. We can call them "cliques" or "groups," but they always develop and can cause social pain—the actual or potential threat to one's social connections (Lieberman, 2019). Research has shown that social pain and physical pain take place in the same areas of the brain. The location of activity related to physical pain has long been known, but the location of social pain is a more recent discovery. It is interesting to note that we use much the same language to describe our social pain as we use to describe our physical pain: "You broke my heart," "My heart aches," "You hurt my feelings." Think about those students who are upset and tell you they have a headache or a stomachache; their pain is real, but it may not be physical. So when Susie and Johnny break up, someone is going to have a broken heart. That's like having a broken leg. It hurts. And according to Lieberman (2019), the brain activity that occurs when someone is sad is calmed by the common painkiller acetaminophen!

Most of the time, students suffer from social pain as a result of rejection. Even in classrooms where everyone seems to work well together, if some students are unable to sit at the "right" table at lunch, are ignored on the bus, or can't play a sport well, they're in pain. And they aren't going to be able to use their cognitive skills because their brain is too busy. In fact, their working memory, which allows them to make decisions, find answers, and do all the other kinds of higher-level thinking, is basically blocked.

When I visit schools and ask when social hierarchy first rears its ugly head, the most common answer is kindergarten! I doubted this until my 5-year-old granddaughter Emmie came home after school in tears because she wasn't invited to Sophia's birthday party. Sophia had handed out her invitations in the classroom, which is OK only when you invite everyone.

"This, too, shall pass." That's what my mom told me. And that observation is usually correct—unless it isn't. Those kids who aren't invited to a party—or worse, to be in a "group"— usually get over it and find something else to dwell on. But what if they don't? The brain shows the effect via the neurotransmitter serotonin, which is released when there is a feeling of social importance or admiration— as when a student is lauded for reaching a goal or just "doing a good job" (Issa, Drummond, Cattaert, & Edwards, 2012; Sinek, 2014). The key is acceptance and belonging. When students are rejected, their serotonin levels are lower, which can lead to feeling stress and making poor choices.

Let's talk about clicks and cliques. A *click* is a group of students who have something in common, such as participating in a sport or music or theater. They "click." They don't spend every moment together, but they support one another in whatever endeavor they have in common. A *clique,* by contrast, is based on power and personality (Hartwell-Walker, 2018). The group expectations may be high, but the security level is low. You never know when you're going to be "out."

There are kids on the fringe who don't really know *where* they belong (they don't fit the profile exactly) or if they *want* to belong to a certain group. Some surveys show teens describing a myriad of cliques or clicks, such as "the jocks," "the brains," "the populars," "the socials," "the gamers"—the list goes on. The research on these groups shows that the students in cliques are much more insecure than the students in clicks. Clicks are friendship groups; cliques are power groups. We want our kids to be in social circles that support their interests, their strengths, and their emotional needs—in other words, the clicks.

It's always good to have a conversation about the social hierarchy with your students. I often created a *sociogram* (a graphic representation of social links that a person has) with my students. Do one at the beginning of the year and again after the New Year; it's usually quite interesting to see who remains friends, and you can gain important information about your students' emotional well-being as well. I also used S. E. Hinton's book *The Outsiders* with my 7th graders to explore clicks and cliques.

Emotional Contagion

As you'll recall from Chapter 2, the brain has mirror neurons that fire when we see someone perform an action or when we experience another's emotion. It is the mirror neuron system that makes emotions contagious. Desautels and McKnight (2019) share a lesson that begins with displaying pieces of chocolate candy. After all the students have seen the candy, the teacher or another person picks up one piece and begins to eat and enjoy it. Then the students are asked to describe what they are seeing and experiencing. The objective is to let students realize that they are experiencing the same feelings as the teacher—emotional feelings such as joy, as well as physical responses. Are their mouths watering? Can they almost taste the chocolate themselves? From this lesson, students should see how they are affected by the actions and emotions of others.

From another perspective, we know that when the teacher is happy, the students sense that happiness and become happy, too. If the teacher becomes upset, it will affect the emotions of each person nearby. The emotion will change the brain state of each student.

Students need to realize that social awareness means not only being aware of others' emotions but also controlling their own emotions in the presence of others; that the classroom and school community are affected by the mirror neuron system and the emotions of each person nearby. This is a time to reinforce students' brain-regulation strategies. You might make a list on the board of strategies students share. How do they regulate their emotions in the presence of someone who is experiencing strong negative emotions? Can they help? Share ways that you deal with those students in the classroom—for instance, taking a whole-class brain break, using the calming area, or saying validating statements (this is where empathy comes in). Have students come up with validating and invalidating statements. For example, instead of saying, "You are overreacting," we can say, "You must really be frustrated." (You can refer to the if/then statements at the end of Chapter 2 for ideas.)

You can also make an academic connection. Describing and defining emotional contagion can be part of a lesson. In English language arts, discuss characters whose emotions affect others. In history, talk about how the emotions of certain key figures (for example, Adolf Hitler, Abraham Lincoln, Fidel Castro, John F. Kennedy) affected others. In science, you can refer to individuals who made breakthroughs only after many failed experiments and roadblocks. How would their emotions have affected others? Mathematicians have been overlooked for their contributions, but Alan Turing is a good example to bring up. Students will relate to him because he is the person whose discoveries led to the development of computers. How would he feel today if he could see how his contribution has affected everyday life?

The chocolate lesson described earlier can help students get a sense of what social awareness includes. But using content to illustrate emotional contagion and other aspects of social awareness will make more of an impression. Embedding these ideas into your content area will reinforce the concepts and make the lessons more "emotional"—and therefore, more memorable.

The Role of Empathy

The competencies needed for social awareness make the critical role of empathy obvious. Empathy needs to become a habit—part of our values and norms. We can't just practice empathy on Fridays for

30 minutes. The information in Chapter 2 can apply to any discussion of social awareness. Empathic students understand the needs of others. Stepping into another's shoes and seeing a situation from their perspective is critical to working together and learning more. With the ability to identify facial expressions and gestures and use good listening skills, students will have the tools to understand others, work with others, and even make play more beneficial.

We've all heard that it's better to give than to receive, and neuroscience can now show us that doing so activates the reward system in the brain. We feel good when others like us, respect us, and are friendly to us, and we feel good when we help other people (Lieberman, 2019).

Some of you may have taught your students about empathy using a role-play situation like the "blue eyes versus brown eyes" activity developed in 1968 by 3rd grade teacher Jane Elliott. As recounted by Bland (2018), it was the day after the assassination of Martin Luther King Jr. Elliott's students had studied King's life and didn't understand why he had been killed. To help them understand, she devised the following experiment. Students are divided into two groups based on eye color, and one group is declared to be superior and deserving of preferential treatment. This group gets more time to finish work, treats, early dismissal, designation as line leaders, and whatever else works for the particular grade level. The other group loses privileges such as drinking from the water fountain and using certain equipment, and those students don't get treats when the other group does. In most cases, the superior group is happier and does better work. When the roles are reversed, the same privileges are given to the superior group and taken away from the other group. Then the debriefing begins, and students share their feelings. Some will be empathic from the beginning, expressing sadness when they see their friends receive lesser treatment. Most students feel so bad as a result of the experience that it brings about a change that is seen at home and at school (Bland, 2018).

When teaching about the Holocaust, many teachers use a similar activity using hair color as the differentiator. Both activities are very powerful. Be aware that some students may react more emotionally than others. It helps if you know everyone's background.

Strategies to Increase Social Awareness

When you provide opportunities for your students to learn how to listen, to relate to the experiences of their classmates and to provide feedback to them, you will be enhancing social awareness. Teaching students how to ask classmates for evidence to support their opinions after giving them the skills and providing modeling in doing so gives them fodder for academic conversations. This type of work improves students' academic skills of analytical thinking and reading, and it relies on social skills like how to handle disagreements and how to have constructive conversations. Prioritizing student discussions over lectures, focusing on strategic thinking rather than coming up with the correct answer, and giving students a chance to learn from their mistakes through productive failure promote higher-level thinking and social skills. The following are some specific strategies for increasing social awareness.

Giving as a Way of Receiving

Arranging for students to give to others, respect differences, and help in school or the community will help them become more socially aware. Setting up a mentoring system in school in which higher-grade students assist lower-grade students is one way of giving. Reminding students about holding doors open for those behind them, helping at home or in the neighborhood by carrying groceries or shoveling snow, and helping with housework all fit this concept as well.

An important component of this type of activity is the feedback that students need. If they get positive feedback reinforcing the idea that what they are doing is helpful and making a difference, they will be inclined to help even more.

Talking Pencils

This simple strategy for discussions follows these four steps:

1. Put students in groups of four.
2. Pose a question and ask each student to give an answer. To share an opinion, the student must place their pencil in the center of the group.
3. Provide sentence frames to help with the discussion. You might use frames such as "I believe my answer is correct because _____," or "I agree with _____ because _____."
4. After the first student speaks, another student can put their pencil in the middle, but they must begin their response with, "Thank you, _____. I don't disagree with what you said, but what about _____?" or "I like your answer. I disagree, however, and this is why."

These sentence frames teach students how to discuss topics in a kind way, allowing for differences in opinion. Cruise the room and listen for kind, respectful talk.

Think-and-Feel-Alouds

The name of this strategy may sound strange, but it's just a think-aloud that expresses feelings. Students are often taught how a skilled reader constructs meaning from text by listening to teachers share their thought processes as they read and think about a portion of script. For SEL purposes, and social awareness in particular, the teacher expresses predictions, understanding, and conclusions drawn from a social interaction. All learning is emotional; group work is both social and emotional. The more awareness there is of the other person's feelings, the more likely it is that a good working relationship will be established. And relationships come first!

For example, when students are going to be working in pairs, a teacher might show students her thought process during an academic conversation to help them focus on their partner's needs. "Devon is having trouble focusing on our assignment. Perhaps I should ask if anything is bothering him. He seems to understand that we have a limited time to complete our task. Maybe I can make this more fun by suggesting we draw pictures of our final project and sort of start with the end in mind. I love to draw, and I'll find out if he does, too!"

Discussing how these thoughts are sensitive to Devon's feelings and whether a student would appreciate if their partner were also trying to understand their own feelings can be a less time-consuming approach to working with a partner than going through a step-by-step process. But if you prefer a more explicit way of teaching, you can suggest students follow these steps:

1. Consider your partner's motivation level.
2. Think of ways to help your partner focus.
3. Be mindful of your partner's feelings throughout your work on this project.
4. Tell your partner when you are feeling good about your work together.
5. Reflect on your social awareness of this interaction.

The Many Roles We Have

Walk into your classroom with name tags on various places on your body. On each tag, write a role that you play. For instance, I would write *mother, wife, teacher, student, sister, daughter, cheerleading coach, student council advisor, bridge player,* and *book lover.*

When students enter the room, I don't have to say anything about my words; the students will instantly ask questions and look at me in a funny way, and someone will almost always try to take one of the tags off. That's when I talk about how each one of those labels is part of who I am. Sometimes I am acting, thinking, and feeling like a mom, sometimes as a teacher, and sometimes as a friend. Each of these is part of who I am.

Like me, students also have "roles" that they step into. We start to talk about their roles. I might give them labels or masking tape on which to write their own labels. If there is time available, after they write their labels, I have them put them on their bodies and we walk around the room "reading" one another. This is an opportunity for students to become aware of who we are, and then we discuss how those roles feel. It's a social awareness discussion. Remind students that they are teachers as well as students, as we all learn from one another. Follow up this activity with reminders when they come in the room next time of who they are and who you need them to be (e.g., "I know you are Cathy's friend, and now I need you to be a student").

Greeting Fellow Students by Name

The more you model this greeting strategy, the easier it will be for your students to follow suit. If students are not accustomed to being called by name, using others' names may feel awkward initially. If they are used to you doing so, the brain begins to identify with the pattern. Ask your students, "Did you know that everyone's favorite word is their name?" I tell my students that although I never liked my name when I was growing up, hearing our name is music to our ears. In fact, research (Carmody & Lewis, 2006) tells us that certain areas of the brain are activated when we hear our own name as opposed to someone else's. Students may not need to know the neurobiology, but it's good to have the information on hand. Which areas of the brain are activated? Those related to self, such as the medial prefrontal cortex. You can tell students to think of this as a direct line to another person's feeling of belonging, a sense of connection. Encourage students to use their classmates' names when seeing them and engaging in conversation with them. Instead of "Hey! What's going on?" say "Kaitlyn! What's going on?" It's likely that more conversation will occur through this "name calling."

Body Language: Gestures and Other Body Movements

Research has confirmed that using gestures when we teach makes lessons more memorable (Clough & Hilverman, 2018). Being aware of body language when others speak can provide information that is not included in the words that are spoken. One great example of this occurs when someone says, "I went fishing yesterday and caught two fish." If no gestures are involved, the statement is informational. But if the speaker holds their hands apart indicating the size of the fish, the statement becomes more interesting and even more informational.

Watching body movements and gestures can help students increase their social awareness. Often, when students become angry or fearful, their body language changes. With students at any grade level, it is worthwhile to talk about what "body language" is and does. The body provides information to enhance the conversation. Accentuate the body language that you use when teaching and ask your students to watch and translate what those movements are "saying" to them. Challenge them not only to use more body language but also to observe it in others.

People Watching: Facial Expressions

Not all facial expressions are created equal. How people express certain feelings on their faces depends on the individual. It is important, however, to discuss some basic facial expressions and what we think they convey in terms of what others are feeling.

We seem to recognize others' facial expressions in an instant, and we draw conclusions based on them. So asking your students to do some people watching, either in real life or through various media, can add to classroom discussions. You can incorporate such discussions in any content area, sometimes asking students to speculate in cases where the answer isn't explicit. Some suggestions follow.

- **In ELA:** How did Wilbur look when Charlotte died in *Charlotte's Web?* How did you look when you read about it? What were Sophie's facial expressions when she had to make a choice in the book *Sophie's Choice?* Authors often provide subtle information (e.g., what characters say and how they behave) that helps the reader understand characters.
- **In history:** What were Napoleon's facial expressions at Waterloo?
- **In science:** How did Willis Carrier look when he realized he had invented the air conditioner? How do you look when you enter an air-conditioned environment after being outside on a hot summer day?
- **In math:** How do you look when you have finished a problem showing all your work and you are done with your homework? What is your facial expression when you know you worked the problem correctly?

More broadly, consider asking your students the following questions, perhaps using them as writing prompts for journals or quick-writes.

- How can you tell when one of your friends is sad or having a bad day?
- What can you do to help someone else when you notice she is "not her usual self"?
- How can you help others feel more included?

- What's a way to help others feel like they belong?
- Why is it so important to be in tune with other people's thoughts and feelings?

Social Media

I would be remiss if I did not bring up social media as an area of increasing importance for social-emotional learning, particularly in terms of empathy. Our students have a large presence on social media. Much communication occurs through platforms such as Instagram, Facebook, Snapchat, and Twitter. And we can't forget text messaging and e-mailing (although the latter has lost its allure for many students, some still use it). Are students aware of the dangers of social media?

Faceless messages can be dangerous. Without information derived from facial expression, tone of voice, and body language, it is so easy to misinterpret a message. Students need some social norms for messaging and for social media. The following are some suggestions drawing from a Common Sense Media report (James, Weinstein, & Mendoza, 2019).

For all students:

1. Protect yourself and your information.
2. Respect others through your use of media.
3. Trust your "gut" to stay safe.
4. Stand up to cyberbullying.
5. Balance your time between using media and your other activities.

For middle and high school students: did you take a photo of friends? Want to share it? Ask yourself,

1. Would my friend agree?
2. Could it get my friend into trouble or cause drama?

3. Am I aware that anyone can share it?
4. Would I be OK with my grandma seeing it?
5. In a year, will I feel good about making this public?

In years past, if something embarrassing happened to us, it might be talked about for a few days, but then some other student would become the butt of a joke. Our embarrassment was hurtful, but it didn't appear to follow us around forever. Today, something can turn up online that will persist for the rest of a student's life. Taking a video of a student falling, arguing, kissing, or something more devastating can be shared among entire student bodies and cause shame or guilt, not to mention anger and a loss of self-regulation.

The hope is that if we have taught empathic behavior, fewer of these situations will occur. But students need frequent reminders that social media is not meant to provide power; it is a means to interact socially with friends, to learn more about the world, and to help those with special needs connect with others if they are unable to do so face-to-face. In an article on this topic, Bradley (2017) states,

> Since most online communities encourage feedback and dialogue, our students need to first learn how to do so in person. Do we teach them how to disagree respectfully? Or to offer kind and constructive feedback? Does empathy drive our students' design thinking? If we don't teach empathy and respect in our classroom communities, how can we expect students to practice them online? (para. 15)

The message is clear: we need to take the time (or *make* the time) to teach our students respectful use of media, create our own norms for the situation, and model the respect and empathic behavior we want to see in them.

Listening to Understand and Show Respect

We can help students hone their ability to be respectful and actively listen through explicit instruction and practice in the following skills:

- Using appropriate eye contact
- Regulating thoughts to limit distractions
- Using facial expressions to message
- Providing appropriate oral responses

Questions that link social awareness and listening skills could include the following:

- Did I listen actively to the person who was talking?
- Was I distracted by something else?
- Did I ask appropriate, respectful, and relevant questions?
- Did I understand the message of that conversation?
- Did my tone of voice and body language appropriately convey how I was feeling?
- Did I respond respectfully and appropriately to someone else's feelings?

Think, Pair, Share

The popular Think, Pair, Share strategy has many variations, and we can add some clear social awareness targets as our students discuss content together. A specific prompt or talking point can be helpful when initiating conversations that include social-emotional learning strategies. The following are suggestions for each component of the strategy.

1. **Think:** As you ready yourself for this conversation, keep in mind your feelings on the topic and the feelings of your partner.

2. **Pair:** You may find yourself with a partner who has a different perspective on the content. Be respectful of your differences.
3. **Share:** Be sure that each of you has equal time to share information.

Discussion Tasks

Academic conversations are class or group discussions that employ critical thinking and higher-level thinking. They allow students to use content knowledge and social awareness skills to deepen learning. To successfully engage in such conversations, the class should be deep enough into the content that they can easily refer to text or other references to prove their own points and build on classmates' information. Social awareness skills that are demonstrated include listening, being respectful of other's time and ideas, looking at information from another's perspective, and working collaboratively. We can look again at this strategy when we move on to relationship building in Chapter 6.

Learning Targets and Social Awareness

Working with Rick Stiggins and his colleagues (Stiggins, 2017) led me to appreciate the importance of providing students of all ages with learning targets. At the time, I was concerned with academic targets only. Now that we realize the importance of the SEL competencies, we can add some SEL learning targets to our list. Doing so makes SEL more explicit to students and helps us keep our focus on the important point that social-emotional learning and academic success are interdependent. Using either *I* or *we* statements may be helpful in personalizing the targets. Here are some examples:

- We can practice active listening as we build on the ideas of others.
- We can make sure that all voices are heard.

- We can practice our norms of _____.
- We can be aware of the feelings of others and how they affect the discussion.

Every Student Has a Story

In *Navigating SEL from the Inside Out,* Stephanie Jones and colleagues (2017) state that students who can successfully manage their behavior and thinking can have better academic achievement. Students with strong social skills will have better relationships and more friendships and be more engaged in learning. Some students will need more direction than others until social awareness becomes automatic. If your students understand social awareness, you will know by the way they "size up" situations and use the information to understand and work together with others. Consider the following if/then statements.

If...	Then...
You have a student who wants to work alone,	Plan enough time to have students figure out how to be a team or cohesive group; do fun group activities to lower stress related to working with others.
A student is placed in a group that has already been formed,	Remind group members of your group norms and ask them to welcome the new member.
Tension has emerged in an ongoing group,	Sit with the group and guide them in coming to a consensus on their project or assignment.

If...	Then...
A student in a group is having some conflict,	Ask if they have tried to understand the others' points of view.
Students in a group have gotten to know one another,	Check to see if they can predict one another's feelings and reactions and recognize individual and group similarities and differences.
One or more group members need assistance,	Help them identify and use resources from their families and their communities, as well as from school.
There is any question about appropriateness related to social media,	Refer students to the norms you have set up and discuss the possibilities and consequences of something unsuitable being added to their digital footprint.

6

Relationship Skills

When children learn more about one another, and when they know their teachers recognize and celebrate their differences, they are more likely to feel a sense of community in the classroom. Teachers foster mutual respect when they provide activities that encourage conversation, sharing, and interaction.

—Fred Rogers

Sally was the newest member of the faculty. She had begun teaching 15 years ago but took off some years to raise her children. When Sally returned to teaching, she was expecting students to have changed considerably in the intervening decade. Interestingly enough, although she conducted her classes in the same manner she had a decade prior, her students were relatively easy to handle, paid attention in class, and had a general grasp of the content. Sally's classroom was neat and tidy. She liked the desks in perfect rows, the bulletin boards bright and inviting, and the markers for the whiteboard lined up on the ledge. Life was pretty good.

But as Sally walked down the hall during her prep period, she noticed that other classrooms were not at all like hers. Students were sitting in groups with desks shoved together haphazardly, and some students were sitting on the floor working. Back-to-School Night was in a few weeks, and she thought the school was going to look unkempt with these disorderly setups.

When it was time for Sally's principal to visit her room, she asked to observe on a day when the students were doing cooperative learning. Sally asked some other teachers about this, and they explained that their students did most of their work in groups. They were more motivated this way and learned more. Sally was also told that cooperative learning made it easier to differentiate instruction, as students could work on components of a project or problem at their own level and pace.

After giving it some thought, Sally decided to follow suit and use learning groups in her classroom. The idea seemed simple: group the students (neatly, in her room!), provide a task, and let them work together. And cooperative learning was not a new strategy, after all. So she jumped right in, eager to see how much her students liked working together as well as how much they learned.

As you might imagine, Sally was in for a shock. Utter chaos took over the classroom. Students fought over responsibilities and interrupted one another constantly. By the end of the day, Sally was in tears... and ready to quit her job!

Fortunately, Tracy, the SEL coach, came to the rescue. She assured Sally that this was a bump in the road, and there were many things she could do to make group work doable and worthwhile. She shared cooperative learning and SEL strategies, explaining that most other teachers wove SEL strategies into their lessons and that Sally's students needed to build skills to handle relationships with their peers. Collaborators were not born; they were made.

This chapter is about learning how to simply handle relationships with others in the classroom and in life. Well, maybe it's not so simple. According to CASEL, the necessary skills include the ability to establish and maintain healthy and rewarding relationships with diverse individuals and groups, to communicate clearly, to listen well, to cooperate with others, to resist inappropriate social pressure, to negotiate conflict constructively, and to seek and offer help when needed—hardly a simple undertaking. But it's important to remember that it all gets easier with age and development. It also gets better if students have the first three SEL competencies—self-awareness, self-management, and social awareness—established. In other words, handling relationships requires first knowing your own emotions, regulating them, and being aware of others' emotions.

In this chapter, we'll look at the topic of handling relationships in terms of the following elements: collaboration, communication, and relationship building—keeping in mind that there is considerable overlap among them. Strategies for one component could well apply to another component.

Relationships in the Brain

It's no surprise that the same brain areas involved in creating teacher-student relationships, as described in Chapter 1, are activated when we teach our students to build, maintain, and restore relationships among themselves. The prefrontal cortex areas related to trust, love, and friendship are engaged through activities that encourage relationships. The *superior temporal sulcus* and the *temporoparietal junction* are involved in social awareness as parts of the system that helps us detect and recognize the purpose of a social interaction. Because the brain is purposed for social interaction— that is, relationships—there is little doubt that these interactions, which are indicative of cooperative learning, are useful and pleasing to the brain. Research has also confirmed a role for the *orbital prefrontal cortex*, which stores information related to relationships; it has been found that this structure is larger in people who have many social interactions and many friends (Pappas, 2012). (See Figure 6.1.)

Figure 6.1
Handling Relationships in the Brain

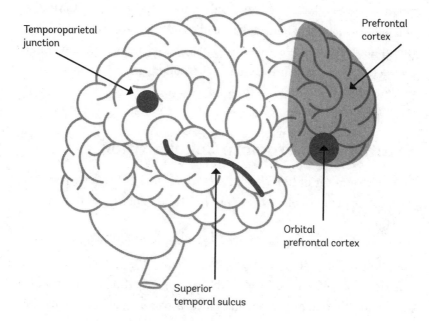

Temporoparietal junction

Prefrontal cortex

Orbital prefrontal cortex

Superior temporal sulcus

The brain chemicals dopamine, noradrenaline, oxytocin, endorphins, and serotonin are also called to action as students move from viewing their peers as classmates to viewing them as teammates. The role of dopamine merits some additional attention. As stated earlier in this book, dopamine is released as we work toward a goal. It is also released when we make a friend. In both children and adolescents, a certain level of dopamine is flowing through the nervous system at all times, and an additional amount is released when they accomplish a feat. However, adolescents' baseline amount is lower than children's, and the additional release amount is higher. As a result, adolescents are primed to encourage an increased release of dopamine, and one way to do that is through novelty. The possibly positive outcome—felt through the additional release of dopamine—is why many adolescents like to try new things and avoid the old. (Daniel Siegel [2014] tells us that the lure of novelty is the only way to get older children to finally leave home!) Herein lies the problem: when adolescents do the same old things, they get bored. Middle and high school teachers: take heed! The kids are bored because they need dopamine. Strategies that release dopamine and other feel-good neurotransmitters have the added benefit of increasing student achievement.

Strategies to Promote Collaboration

Jo Boaler, author of *Limitless Mind* (2019), says, "When we connect with other people's ideas there are multiple benefits for our brains and for our lives."

Learning can be lonely. When students run into trouble understanding a concept or working a problem, they sometimes give up. However, when working with a group of students, they have someone other than the teacher to turn to for questions, problem solving, and academic conversations.

Opportunities for collaboration come in many different forms. Cooperative learning groups and myriad other strategies are well known and popular. Of course, some setups have students seated together at tables or in small groups of desks, but no collaboration takes place. Collaboration is less a physical grouping and more an intellectual interaction, a peer-coaching situation, or a high-challenge/low-threat opportunity to stretch student thinking through bouncing ideas off one another.

We have all encountered "new" strategies through professional development that have quickly fallen by the wayside because they don't work well enough for our situations. The strategies I offer here, however, are research based and brain compatible, and they have withstood the test of time. They work because they engage students and develop the relationships that enable student success. They also allow us to teach social, emotional, and cognitive skills surreptitiously.

We know from John Hattie's (2017) research that direct (teacher-centered) instruction does work, with an effect size of .60. However, if direct instruction is our only approach to teaching, the routine and predictability may *calm* the brain without always *engaging* the brain. Direct instruction also doesn't provide the opportunity for students to interact and learn social skills such as how to handle relationships. The following strategies offer a variety of ways to both engage the brain and teach relationship skills.

Teaming

I cannot say enough about the effectiveness of teaming, which I began using regularly early in my career. Teaming can solve a number of problems and achieve various purposes, from the minor (it makes taking attendance easier) to the significant (it can make teaching and learning more fun; enable students to give one another positive feedback that may increase their serotonin levels, which may make them calmer and happier; and give them a feeling of belonging, which is one of the basic needs). It also enables students to learn and practice the emotional and social skills that are necessary for success in school and in life—including the team-oriented world of business and other professions.

Teaming can give students a group to be with as they enter the room. When I take attendance, I say, "If you have 100 percent of your team members seated and ready to go, raise your hand and say 'Yes!'" They have to check and make sure that their teammates are present. It gives kids a good feeling to know that people are going to notice when they aren't there. Team members might collaborate on homework, remind one another of upcoming assignments, and keep one another on task.

There are numerous methods for putting teams together. If you are forming academic teams that will work together throughout the year, during an entire semester, or on a given project, it is important to make the teams as diverse as possible in terms of culture, skills, and even personalities. The most recent research suggests that we make the teams small—between two and five students. Mixed gender is also a consideration as we prepare students to work collaboratively in the real world (Toth & Sousa, 2019).

Depending on grade level and purpose, you might take some simple steps to give teams an identity and enable them to operate effectively. Some suggestions follow.

1. Develop team norms. Teams need norms to guide their work and keep everyone on task. Examples might include *Work cooperatively, Take turns speaking, Listen carefully,* and *Be polite.* You can help individual teams come up with their norms, or the entire class can work together to develop norms that all teams will follow.

Discussing potential problems and role-playing ways to address them may be necessary if your students have not previously experienced a team-type learning situation. With your help, students can come up with answers to questions that almost always come up, such as the following:

- What do we do when a student is absent? (Assign the task to another team member.)
- What if we are having trouble understanding what to do? (Send out "spies" to see what the other teams are doing.)

- What should we do if our discussion turns into an argument? (Take a break!)
- How should we deal with a team member who is fooling around? (Refer to your norms! Ask the teacher if necessary.)

2. Pick a team name. Students typically identify sports teams with names, so this step may be fun. Make sure they keep the names positive and noncontroversial, and if you like, they may be associated with a specific topic. Within the team, individuals may have titles or roles. For example, I have assembled teams with each member identified by the name of a different character from *The Wizard of Oz*. The character has specific tasks to take care of for the team. What I find compelling about this strategy is the ability to get students to quickly accomplish specific tasks. For instance, I may say, "OK, I need all the Dorothys to come up and count out enough assignment sheets for the team."

3. Devise a team scorecard or chart. On a sheet of plain paper or a larger sheet of construction paper, students can create a scorecard or chart to use for self-assessment. Team members may assess themselves, using a scale of 1 through 10, on such criteria as cooperation, participation, punctuality, and homework completion, as shown in the sample chart in Figure 6.2. (Remember, this is only an example. Be creative!)

4. Assign roles. Roles such as *facilitator* and *leader* are helpful to keep teams on task. Rather than have students vote for someone to fill the position, let each person decide if they want to be a leader. Perhaps they can take turns. Give them a job description for the role so they know what will be expected. If no team members are interested, you may choose a leader and work with that student on developing leadership qualities. Try to choose someone who already appears to have some good emotional intelligence skills and works well with others. You may be surprised at how well some students do in this capacity. Leadership skills often are not evident because students have not been in situations where they needed to use them. Choosing a leader or facilitator may be a great opportunity to discuss world or local leaders and how they conduct themselves. Perhaps the students could pick one of these well-known and successful leaders to model themselves after.

Figure 6.2
Sample Team Chart

Team	Criteria				Average Team Score on All Criteria
	Cooperation	Participation	Punctuality	Homework	
Dendrites	5	7	10	8	7.5
Brainiacs	7	9	9	8	8.3
Dreamers	6	7	10	9	8
Thinkers	9	10	9	10	9.5

The steps just outlined provide a good starting point for setting up teams. If you have time, you may want to try these additional activities:

- Give the teams some questions to answer as a "getting to know you" activity. We sometimes assume that kids who have gone to school together know one another, but some questions can spur interesting conversations and the sharing of bits of information they didn't know before. Use questions such as these: "Who are three people you would like to have over for dinner tonight?" "Who would you like to see walk in the door right now?" "If you could be anywhere else right now, where would you be?"
- How about some team colors, a team handshake, or a team logo? Discussing and reaching an agreement on these

identifiers will bring the group members together and help make them a cohesive unit.

- Students can make up a cheer or choose a theme song for the team. Doing so enhances the team-identification process and can be loads of fun, and you can have students use the cheer or song to notify you when their team has completed an assignment or a project.

Jill Fletcher (2019) shares the following team activity in an *Edutopia* article. Teams of students use poster paper to create a sheet called a "one-pager" that includes their team name; group favorites, such as food and movies; their favorite meme; and a symbol to represent each member of the group. The one-pager serves as a group flag. Fletcher then takes a picture of each poster and posts the pictures around the room (the posters would take up too much space) to help provide her middle schoolers with a sense of identity and belonging.

It's worth noting that these steps and suggestions are not limited to long-term teams. Several of them, such as "getting to know you" activities, team names, and team cheers or slogans, can also be useful for small groups that will work together on some of the content they are learning. No matter what the size of the team, the sense of belonging that students feel is reflected in the brain, as it releases serotonin for calming and dopamine for focus and engagement.

Project-Based Learning (PBL)

Project-based learning, as opposed to direct instruction, is a teaching method that uses complex real-world problems as the vehicle to promote student learning of concepts and principles. Some norms for PBL include the following:

- The problem must motivate students to seek out a deeper understanding of concepts.

- The problem should require students to make reasoned decisions and to defend them.
- The problem should incorporate the content objectives in a way that connects to previous courses/knowledge.
- When used for a group project, the problem should have a level of complexity that requires the students to work together to solve it.
- When used for a multistage project, the initial steps of the problem should be open-ended and engaging to draw students into the problem. (Drawing students into the problem causes the release of dopamine, which keeps the brain focused.)

Project-based learning promotes social-emotional learning at every grade level. Collaboration is at the heart of PBL, so students must have relationship skills to make this a pleasant and memorable learning experience. Goal setting, organizational skills, self-motivation, teamwork, listening skills, and conflict resolution all come into play as students manage projects and meet deadlines. If conflict arises—and it often does—students practice their emotional management skills and work together to resolve the issue. Of course, the teacher is monitoring throughout and may need to step in to help negotiate a solution.

Cooperative Learning

According to teacher and neurologist Judy Willis (2012), "Brain research tells us that adolescents experience more comfort and enjoyment when pleasurable social interaction is incorporated into their learning experiences. 'Inclusion' in this context refers to a sense of belonging to a group where a student feels valued and begins to build resiliency" (para. 4).

The brain learns best when we are interacting, talking, and collaborating. Talking activates the prefrontal cortex, where higher-level thinking takes place. But there is more to cooperative learning than putting students in groups and having them talk through situations and projects. Most students don't know how to work collaboratively. According to Johnson, Johnson, and Smith (2013), the following five elements are what enable successful small-group learning.

- **Positive interdependence:** Students feel responsible for their own and the group's effort.
- **Face-to-face interaction:** Students encourage and support one another; the environment encourages discussion and eye contact.
- **Individual and group accountability:** Each student is responsible for doing their part; the group is accountable for meeting its goal.
- **Group behaviors:** Group members gain direct instruction in the interpersonal, social, and collaborative skills needed to work with others.
- **Group processing:** Group members analyze their own and the group's ability to work together.

Jigsaw

The jigsaw strategy is a research-based cooperative learning technique for group work and a wonderful way to learn material. It was created in 1971 by Eliot Aronson and his graduate students, who were providing assistance to a school in Austin, Texas. The desegregation of schools had led to tension among the white, African American, and Hispanic students. The kids didn't trust one another, and they had preconceived notions about their abilities. The jigsaw strategy has been shown to reduce racial conflict and improve educational outcomes, including higher test scores, reduced absenteeism, and greater interest in school (Aronson, 2000).

In the jigsaw approach, students are divided into diverse groups and assigned distinct tasks under a common topic. Students become independent experts on their subtopic and work with leaders of the same task from other groups. Then each person returns and teaches their original group about their area of expertise. Everyone becomes an important information resource using this strategy, and students learn about empathy and engagement as they realize that everyone in the group and in the classroom is interdependent. Here are the steps for creating a "jigsaw classroom":

1. Divide students into diverse groups of five or six.
2. Assign a group leader.
3. Divide your lesson into five or six sections.
4. Assign a section to each student in the group.
5. Give students time to look over the text and read it—and reread it!
6. Form "expert" groups by having the students from each group with the same assignment gather together.
7. After the expert groups discuss their topic and conclude that they all know it sufficiently, have students return to their original groups.
8. Ask each student to share their expertise to teach the others in their group about their section.
9. Move around the room and check on the groups.
10. When the jigsaw session is over and it appears that all students understand the information, give them a quiz and show them how much they have learned.

Strategies for Communication

Communication skills, both oral and written, are obviously a key component in teaching students how to handle relationships. In today's tech-dominant world, students can even benefit from instruction in a decidedly non-tech and seemingly "natural" form of communication: face-to-face conversation. Written communication is equally important, and its many forms can play an important role as students develop—and reflect on—their relationship skills.

No Phone, New Friends Friday

At Iowa Valley Junior-Senior High School in Marengo, Iowa, principal Janet Behrens was concerned that students were not developing face-to-face communication skills because they were always buried in their phones (Kennon, 2019). She began the tradition of No Phone, New Friends Friday, a phone-free lunch hour in which students get to meet and talk to other students whom they may not know. As students enter the cafeteria, they are given a color-coded card that represents the table at which they will sit. Conversation starters are provided at the tables. The students believe they have a friendlier and kinder school because they know one another better.

Journaling After Cooperative Learning or Teamwork

Asking students to write in their journals after a cooperative learning project, a teaming project, or a jigsaw offers some individual time for reflection. You can provide prompts such as these:

- Did my group reach its goals?
- How did I feel while working on this project?
- How much did I participate in the project?
- Do I feel good about my participation and the accomplishments of the group?

Keep in mind that while they are journaling, the students are reviewing the actual material and concepts you want them to remember and transfer to other situations. Journaling can be a memory tool.

Role Playing

Role playing is very helpful in teaching students communication skills, encouraging social engagement, and fostering respectful interaction: students learn how to respond in a variety of situations and get valuable practice using those responses. Role-playing scenarios also activate emotions, teach students how to control impulses, and allow students to see situations from different perspectives. As in a debate, students can switch roles and support an argument from their opponent's point of view.

In addition, the strategy can be used in any content area to rehearse and reinforce learning. For example, students might role-play an interaction between soldiers from the North and South during the Civil War, a discussion between x and y in an algebra problem, or an amusing conversation between a beaker and a Bunsen burner during a science experiment. During these scenarios, the prefrontal cortex is engaged as students' brains use long-term memories and prior knowledge to reinforce their roles.

Cortisol, dopamine, and oxytocin are all released because role playing is like storytelling in that it involves excitement, curiosity, challenge, and connection.

Strategies for Relationship Building

Strategies that build relationships show students how to interact in ways in which there is "serve and return"—that is, back-and-forth interactions that help students get to know one another better and work together respectfully. Here are some relationship-building strategies to add to your toolbox.

Brainstorming

Brainstorming is an excellent way to promote relationship building, because it requires a variety of social-emotional skills, including careful listening, taking turns speaking, prioritizing ideas, and respectfully communicating with others. You can use brainstorming as either a small-group or a whole-class activity. It can be content related (e.g., coming up with possible answers to questions about specific content or thinking of ways to demonstrate knowledge, such as presentations, infomercials, or performance assessments) or more general in nature (e.g., coming up with ideas for a school dance or the best ways to communicate with parents).

You can provide one or more statements or questions to launch the brainstorming. It will work best if you have guidelines for the brainstorming session. Because students may think of a brainstorming session as a free-for-all in which they can just shout out ideas, assigning roles will be helpful. For example, choose a note taker to jot down each idea, a timekeeper to track responses and keep contributions within the allotted time, and a taskmaster to keep everyone focused on the task at hand. You may also want to provide time to weed out responses that don't lead the group to its goal.

Classroom "Seating Challenges"

When we understand the social-emotional lives of our students, we know that the question "Where do I sit?" is one of their greatest concerns in a new environment. All kinds of classroom seating strategies are possible, from seating students alphabetically to letting them sit wherever they want. As discussed in Chapter 1 and confirmed by Souers and Hall (2016), assigned seating may be comforting to kids, especially those who come to us having faced trauma in their lives.

Teacher Sandy Merz (2012) came up with some great ideas to answer the "Where do I sit?" question for his 8th graders that can be used for students at any level. In his classroom, students sit at round tables in groups of five. On the first five days of the school year, he uses various seating approaches, which he calls "seating challenges" because the students determine where they sit based on problem-solving exercises. In the process, he gets to know his students and they get to know one another. An important outcome of his strategy is the collaboration that is necessary to complete the activity.

On Day 1, before students can sit down, he greets them at the door and tells them to follow the instructions that are posted clearly for all to see. For example, Day 1's post reads, "Sit in birthday order so that the person whose birthday is closest to January 1 sits in Seat 1. The person in Seat 5 will raise his or her hand when everyone is seated." On the following four days, Merz has other ways for students to be seated, such as "alphabetically according to the name you like to be called" or according to height. Other options, such as seating according to sneaker and non–sneaker wearers or a preference for spending time outdoors or indoors, involve further subdivisions within the group, such as curly or straight hair.

Using Merz's approach, you can get to know a lot about your students and they about their classmates. The method is fun and different, and the 10 or 15 minutes it takes each day is forgivable at the beginning of the year or semester.

Assigned Seating at Lunch

A lunchtime idea being used in a K–12 school in Wisconsin eliminates the question "Who am I going to eat lunch with?" Students from different grade levels are assigned seats at round tables of eight, plus a teacher. The teacher gets the students talking to one another, which is especially helpful for new kids, and the seating assignments rotate periodically (Files, 2019).

Some schools have found that assigned lunch seating has helped reduce bullying. As kids get to know one another, relationships improve, and as one "bully" said to me, "It's harder to hurt someone you know." Social-emotional learning and trauma-informed practices can help bullies understand why their actions hurt and intimidate others, but they also serve our desire to protect all our students.

Getting to know one another over a meal is standard practice in many cultures. Using lunchtime for positive social interactions provides an opportunity to model appropriate behaviors, such as respecting others (including those who are different from ourselves), listening, showing empathy, and finding common ground.

Restorative Practices and Peacemaking Circles

If the game Rock Paper Scissors worked as a conflict resolution strategy, would you use it? Could it be that easy? Michele Borba (2016) saw its effectiveness at recess based on a program called Playworks. The Playworks organization helps schools deal with the difficulties that some children experience during recess for various reasons. Playworks helps schools figure out what works well on their playground, an area that may be the only outdoor space where kids feel safe and can play. They focus on safety, engagement, and empowerment, incorporating conflict resolution, leadership, fairness, and good sportsmanship into the plan. Some of the Chicago Public Schools are using this national program to assist with the social-emotional needs of their students. Playworks president Elizabeth Cushing says, "Play is not just a fun activity kids happen to do. It's a developmentally critical behavior through which kids learn" (Tate, 2019, para. 9). When the inevitable conflict occurs, students may use Rock Paper Scissors to resolve the issue. When playing outdoors, kids want to "get back to the game" as quickly as possible, so with minor incidents, "rocking it out" is swift and easy.

Restorative practices can come into play with other kinds of conflicts both in and out of class, replacing punitive disciplinary practices with strategies to build community and repair relationships that have been damaged by conflict. This approach depends on social-emotional skills as students must recognize their own emotions, control them, recognize the emotions of the other student in the conflict, and then work to solve the problem. With restorative practices, those who have been harmed and those who have done harm are brought together to elicit actions that can repair the relationship.

As Sally, from the chapter's opening scenario, learned about the importance of group work and how to teach her students the skills of handling relationships, she also found the need to learn more about restorative practices. Several situations arose in her class that led to apparently broken relationships owing to irreconcilable differences. In one incident, for example, two classmates seemed unable to work together without bickering, leading to hurt feelings and anger. Sally hoped to restore their relationship, and she wanted both students to be heard. The key was making sure each understood how the other felt. They needed to see the situation from each other's perspective, which would be possible only if they could first control their own emotions and recognize the other's emotions. Sally and the students discussed how their tone of voice, body language, and gestures might provide clues as to how they were feeling. With that kind of background information, they could move on to the particulars of restorative justice, which is just one part of *restorative practices*.

Srinivasan (2019) describes restorative practices as "specific practices inspired by indigenous values that build community, respond to harm or conflict, and provide circles of support for community members" (para. 11). An interesting practice called "classroom circles" involves students forming a circle (sometimes standing, sometimes sitting). It is strongly suggested that the first few times you form a circle with your class, you do so simply to build relationships and a sense of community, and to help students feel safe. You can come to the circle to cocreate classroom goals, values, and norms, and later to revisit these classroom elements. When the class is comfortable with this process, you can move on to using the circle for other purposes, such as conflict resolution for incidents like the one between Sally's two students.

A behavioral disorder can prompt the use of *restorative conversations*. These conversations are based on questions such as *What happened?* (rather than *What did you do?*), *What were you thinking* (at the time)? *What are you thinking now? Who was harmed? How can we repair it?*

One way to initiate a restorative conversation is through the use of a "peacemaking circle," in which the class (including the teacher) gathers and listens to the victim and the offender and tries to help find a way for the offender to make up for the harm. Often a mindfulness activity, such as playing meditative music for a few minutes or asking students to sit quietly and focus on a spot on the floor while breathing deeply, begins the circle. The person talking holds an object called a "talking piece," and no one else is allowed to speak until they are holding it. When you begin to use circles, you can start with fun questions like *What's your favorite kind of music?* When students become more comfortable with the process, the questions or talking points can go deeper. This strategy can be used for all grade levels and done in as little as five minutes. Students are not required to join the circle, but I have always been amazed at how many students want to talk. Respect, relationships, and community are at the heart of this strategy.

Activities that help students build relationships and community in your classroom can be used in a circle. Here is one activity from *Edutopia* (2014):

> You're in My Boat: Have a student share something personal, such as an experience or something he is interested in, by saying, "You're in my boat if…." For example, "You're in my boat if you like French fries," or "You're in my boat if someone got upset with you this morning." All who agree with the statement get up and change seats; the others remain seated.

This activity is similar to "A River Runs Through Us," described in Chapter 1.

Setting up a restorative-practices school involves much more than what I've described here. For more information, go to http://

schottfoundation.org/sites/default/files/restorative-practices-guide.pdf.

Every Student Has a Story

Teaching students to handle relationships with their peers can be challenging, but they must learn how to work with others, as this ability will affect their future personal and professional relationships. In many cases, peer acceptance is more important to students than academic content. Students who have suffered many ACEs may experience difficulty dealing with peers and feel even greater stress dealing with adults. Trauma may make them feel different or unacceptable to others. Consider the following if/then scenarios when working on relationship building in your classroom.

If...	Then...
Students are causing disruption,	Remind them of the classroom norms (or cocreate some if you have none).
The class is sluggish and learning is slow,	Use collaborative strategies to add energy and enthusiasm, and express excitement about the content. Emotions are contagious!
Students are being left out of teamwork or group work,	Introduce a jigsaw session that will make everyone equal partners in the learning.
Behavior is causing harm to a student,	Try a restorative circle or restorative justice questions to get to the reason for the behavior.

If...	Then...
You and your class require a change and a challenge,	Try using project-based learning to boost learning, interaction, and change.
You realize that teamwork and collaboration are essential to your students' future success,	Use any form of collaboration —such as cooperative learning, project-based learning, or teaming—in your classroom instruction.
You have students who have had traumatic experiences and don't want to work in cooperative groups,	Try paired activities like Think, Pair, Share before assigning students to work in larger groups, and provide more structure to your group activities.

7.

Responsible Decision Making

It is neurobiologically impossible to build memories, engage complex thoughts, or make meaningful decisions without emotion.

—Mary Helen Immordino-Yang

Mr. Beck asked his 5th graders to choose a famous person for a report. They could find a biography or an autobiography, conduct Internet searches, or research their "person" in any other way. He encouraged them to dress like their person on the day of the report and even offered to help them with costumes or hats. He really thought this would be a fun activity.

As he cruised the room to help kids find what they needed for research, he realized the chatter he was hearing relayed not excitement but anxiety. The Brainiac Team was abuzz with chatter. He stopped and listened. He heard, "I don't know who to pick! Who are you going to pick?" "I don't know. What if I pick someone who isn't interesting?" "I know! I was thinking of Eleanor Roosevelt because she was an independent woman for her time, but what if I can't find anything? I give up!"

It was the "I give up!" that sent Mr. Beck reeling. How could students be giving up only minutes after he had given them the assignment? Why couldn't they make up their minds? Why couldn't they try a few possibilities and then land on a choice? He wanted to yell, "Just decide!" And then he realized that was the problem: some of these kids couldn't make a decision.

He considered this issue for a few minutes, cruised once more, and decided to address the entire class. "Students, please give me your attention. How many of you have decided on your person?" (Only a few raised their hands.) "How many of you are having trouble?" (More raised their hands than had done so in response to the first question.)

"Mr. B., why can't you just assign us people?" asked Jessie from the Tartan Team.

"Yeah, just give us a person. Don't make us decide," Juan from the TikTok Team added.

Mr. Beck responded, "I don't think it's the report and presentation that are the problem; it's your decision-making skills. You make decisions every day. Before you got to school, you decided what to wear, what to have for breakfast or whether to have breakfast, what to bring with you to school, and whom to talk to this morning."

"We don't have any food at home, so I didn't get any breakfast. I came to school to eat breakfast," moaned Roger.

"So circumstances helped you make a decision. No food at home; eat at school," Mr. Beck replied (feeling heartsick that Roger didn't have food at home and glad that he felt comfortable enough to share that information).

"My mother always makes a big breakfast; I don't get to make a decision on that!" retorted Keisha.

"So you decided what or how much you would eat of what your mom prepared. You made decisions involving breakfast," Mr. Beck countered.

"I wore what was clean and ironed. No decision making for me!" shouted Ian.

"Sometimes we base our decisions on our circumstances. I'm glad you wore clean clothes!" Mr. Beck smiled as he checked their faces for a glimmer of acknowledgment. Were they getting it?

"Well, you gave us too many choices. I can't decide," declared Jessie.

"Yeah," said Juan, "narrow it down for us. Please!"

"Let's do some team decision making. Discuss together your individual strengths and interests and see if that helps you narrow down your choices. Perhaps you like science best and decide to choose a scientist for your report, or you love literature and decide to choose your favorite author. Try this for 10 minutes. Keep your options open. Narrow it down to a couple of people, so if you have difficulty finding information on one, you can try the other."

Mr. Beck had to extend the time to 15 minutes, but the approach worked. With their teammates, the students each came up with two or three people to begin their research. He thought, "I made a good decision when I had them work with their teams."

Decision making is important to everything students do at school, in every class, from note taking (*How do I decide what to write down?*) to writing an essay (*What's important? What do I want to tell my audience?*) to answering questions on an assessment (*What is the question really asking me? What is the assessment asking of me?*). No matter what you teach, you ask students to choose.

Of course, decisions are at the heart of teachers' lives as well. Teachers make an estimated 1,500 educational decisions every day (Goldberg & Houser, 2017). Imagine if you had to stop and go through a step-by-step process to make each decision! So many of your daily decisions are based on previous experience and emotion. You have considered the steps repeatedly, when you had time to consider the situation, the alternatives, the consequences of each decision, and your ethical or moral responsibility in making the choice. And that's the key word: *choice*.

In the case of Mr. Beck's students, had he not been offering them enough choices? Is that why they had difficulty? Or was it time? Did they feel rushed? Perhaps some truly didn't understand the assignment or had no clue as to what person might be considered famous. Whatever the cause, the point is that decision making can be influenced by many thinking models and thought processes.

SEL and Responsible Decision Making

According to CASEL, responsible decision making is the ability to make constructive choices about personal behavior and social interactions based on ethical standards, safety concerns, and social norms. Students need to evaluate the consequences of their decisions, including their effects on the well-being of not only themselves but also others. Responsible decision making includes identifying problems, analyzing situations, solving problems, evaluating choices, and reflecting on the outcome.

The Heart of Illinois United Way produced a booklet offering decision-making tips to kids (Camden et al., n.d.) that suggests asking the following questions.

Before:

- What is the problem?
- What are two possible solutions?
- What are the consequences of these solutions?
- If both options look like they are going to end badly, what do you do?

After:

- What choice did you make?
- Would you do anything differently?
- Reminder: When you make the wrong decision, you become more resilient as long as you try again.

Or you might go through the following steps (Landmark School Outreach, n.d.):

1. *Identify:* Begin with having students observe their surroundings to notice problems to be solved.
2. *Analyze:* Stop, think, and break the problem down into the component parts.
3. *Solve:* Have students brainstorm possible solutions. Begin with small groups.
4. *Evaluate:* Create an if/then chart *or* a decision-making tree.
5. *Reflect:* How did your choice work for you? If it didn't have a good outcome, how could you have made it better? If it worked well, what would you repeat of the process for future outcomes?

Decision Making in the Brain

Every considered decision we make involves the prefrontal cortex, which, as we know, is a critical part of our thinking brain. According to Sousa (2015), it's the *orbitofrontal* portion of the prefrontal cortex that "regulates our abilities to evaluate, inhibit, and act on social and emotional information" (p. 19). The *ventromedial* and *ventrolateral* portions of the prefrontal cortex are also involved in decision making, as the first deals with risk and the second with goal-appropriate responses (Hiser & Koenigs, 2018). Their response activity will be influenced by the *amygdala* (which is involved in emotions) and the *hippocampus* (which is involved in memory), so our feelings and our previous experiences (memories) will influence the activity in the prefrontal cortex. All this occurs when we make *conscious* decisions; thus, one of the first rules of good decision making is to *slow down and think*. (See Figure 7.1.)

Figure 7.1
Decision Making in the Brain

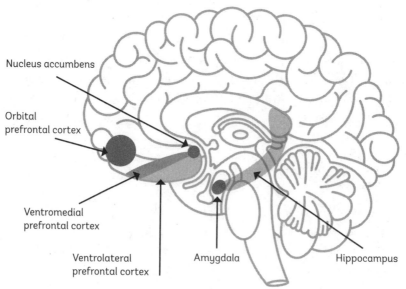

Nucleus accumbens

Orbital
prefrontal cortex

Ventromedial
prefrontal cortex

Ventrolateral
prefrontal cortex

Amygdala

Hippocampus

Dopamine is a reward for good decisions. Good decisions are predictions made using sound information. When we make a prediction and are correct, that good feeling we get is from the *nucleus accumbens* releasing extra dopamine into the prefrontal cortex (McTighe & Willis, 2019). Dopamine is also released as a reward when we make snap decisions that are correct. Our brains desire the "feel-good" chemical and will therefore decide based on anticipation of the rewards they will get.

What happens in the brain when we make split-second decisions? Our emotional brain takes over. In such cases, there is no time to give careful thought through the prefrontal cortex. Our decisions now become based on reflexive responses.

Factors in Decision Making: Time, Values, and Priorities

Several factors play important roles in the decision-making process. These include the time frame for the decision (*Do we need to decide quickly, or can we take time for a more thoughtful approach?*); our values (*How do our beliefs about right and wrong play into the decision?*); and our priorities (*Where does this decision fit in the greater framework of what's going on in our lives?*). Let's examine each of these more closely.

Time

When I arrived at my middle school at 6:30 a.m., I was shocked to see Maya sitting outside the front door. I smiled and asked what she was doing there so early. She looked at me, and the tears started to fall.

"Oh, Mrs. S., I am in so much trouble. I don't know why I did it. I knew after I got there that I had done the wrong thing. But the other girls were laughing and having fun, and I just wanted to fit in."

"Hold up, Maya. I need a bit more information. Give me some background here. What did you do that you regret? What were you doing that you knew was wrong? And why do you think you're in trouble?" I guided her inside the building and to my classroom. I was there early to catch up on work, but I knew Maya needed my undivided attention. I handed her a tissue, sat down on one of the student desks, and waited for her to pull herself together enough to tell her story. She sat across from me, sniffled, and began:

> Yesterday after school, I was supposed to go to Emma's house to work on our science project with her and Danita. I was ready to go, but as I was heading to Emma's mom's car, Elly grabbed my arm and said, "Maya, come with me to Preston's house. We're going over there to listen to music, and I want you to go with me. His parents aren't home. It's going to be so much fun!" When I said I had other plans, she said, "No, please, you have to go with me. I'll be your best friend forever. Besides, all the cool kids are going to be there—don't you want to hang out with them?" So I went. I know I shouldn't have, but I *do* want to be with the cool kids. I figured Emma and Danita would finish the project—actually, I didn't think about the project at all. But thank goodness, Emma saw me get in Elly's dad's car, so she didn't call school or my mom to ask where I was. But I know I'm going to get in trouble today because Danita will tell Mr. Montgomery that I didn't help finish the project. Why am I so stupid?

I said, "So, you're telling me that you made a spur-of-the-moment decision that you now regret?" Moaning, Maya responded, "I had so much fun at Preston's; it felt so good to be with that group that I've never even eaten lunch with before. We made dance videos and watched a movie. The minute I got into Elly's dad's car to go home, I thought I was doomed, but my parents didn't suspect a thing. They were both in the kitchen when I got home. I don't think they remembered exactly what I was doing after school."

"And now it's time for the consequences from your rash decision. What are you going to do? Have you decided how you are going to handle this?" I asked.

"I know Mr. Montgomery is going to be disappointed. But I thought about it all night. I'm going to explain to him that I made other plans by mistake. I'll apologize to Emma and Danita. But I'm wondering if I can get away with not telling my mom and dad. If no one says anything to them, why upset them?"

"You've had time to think about this. Are you going to lie to Mr. Montgomery and avoid telling your parents the truth?"

"Is that bad, Mrs. Sprenger? Am I making another bad choice?"

"You have some time before school starts to think about the consequences of your decision. Is it OK to tell your teacher a lie? I think Mr. Montgomery would understand the truth, even if you have to pay a penalty for your actions. What if your parents eventually find out from one of your friends or their parents? You have a lot to think about, and now you have the chance to make a reflective decision—unlike the reflexive one you made yesterday."

Maya was embroiled in a battle between her need to belong and her conscience. The impulsive decision she made to break plans and go with Elly was made without the benefit of time. When time is on our side, however, we usually make better decisions. Taking the time to look at the big picture and weigh the pros, cons, and consequences of each option generally leads us to the right decision for us. *Generally.*

You are in a hurry to get to the airport to pick up your mother, and you stop by the paint shop to make the final decision on the color of your child's room. As you gaze at the color strips of lavender, teal, and brick red, you realize your mom will land in 20 minutes! You turn to the color consultant at the store and say, "Mix up the lavender. I'll pick it up later," and you dash out to your car. As you drive to the airport, you begin to think about your choice. You start to doubt yourself. Perhaps lavender really won't go well with the bedspread you just bought. Will the sample patch of color that you painted on the bedroom wall really look good in the whole room? Isn't brick red more popular according to home design magazines? And on and on.

At this point, you have shut down the emotional brain and your prefrontal cortex has taken over. Perhaps if you had taken more time, the bedroom would be a very different color!

Some people trust their instincts more than others. What is certain is that having too little time or information to make a decision may lead to an unwanted result.

Values and Priorities

Values are general beliefs about what is right and wrong. Values remain constant, unlike norms, which change depending on the situation. Priorities tell us what is most important to us.

Decision making is based on our values and our priorities at any given time. The process reflects and sharpens our values, bringing them into focus. It is important to discuss values with students, create classroom values, and refer to them when asking students to work on anything that would require making decisions.

Creating a social contract with your class is a good way to discuss and determine classroom values. You can begin by asking the following guiding questions:

- How do you want to be treated by me?
- How do you want to be treated by one another?
- How do you think I want to be treated by you?
- How do you want to handle violations of the contract?

Students can answer the questions independently and then share their responses, which can become the basis for reaching consensus. The consensus then becomes the basis for drawing up a contract that is signed by the students and teacher and posted in the classroom. This process helps students interact and feel heard, and they can begin to monitor themselves according to the contract. The contract itself may consist of the four questions listed with the answers beneath, or it may be a list of behaviors that the class values, such as *Be respectful, Listen carefully, Show empathy, Be kind,* and so on. Schools such as John Haines Elementary School in Chicago are successfully using such contracts (*Edutopia,* 2019b).

No matter what class I teach, I love to talk to students about values and priorities. I believe it's fine to want to be a professional athlete, have an empire like many of the reality show stars, or be a professional—anything, really—but it's important to recognize that there are other priorities in our lives. Students need to be aware that their decisions are based on their priorities, which in turn are based on their values. Take some time to discuss this concept, using activities such as the following.

- Have students write down their entire school day schedule and discuss the implications. How important is it that the schedule be followed? What do the schedules reveal about their choices and priorities?
- Take your daily schedule and mix it up. Ask students to put the schedule in the order they would prefer. This can be a fun activity that connects you to your students as they learn about priorities, plans, and schedules.
- Have students create a "priority grid." A lot of decision making goes into the priority grid activity, and it can help you find out a lot about your students and their present needs. (This activity was created by my colleague and friend Janet Leonard, who works tirelessly with educators on the topics of values and priorities.) Here are the steps:
  1. Have a discussion with students about the difference between a value and a priority.
  2. Give each student two blank pieces of 8 × 10 paper, and ask them to draw a 12-section grid on each piece.
  3. On one piece, have them label the grid with the numbers 1 through 12. Explain that you will be telling them a series

of words or phrases, and on the other piece of paper they should write each word or phrase in one of the grid sections. After they have written the words and phrases, they will tear out each section and place it on the numbered grid on the other sheet of paper according to their belief of its order of importance. Here are 11 of the words and phrases: *having fun, having friends, money, stuff (possessions), looks, family, education, being respected by others, health, being really good at something, staying out of trouble.* The 12th word or phrase can be anything they choose (e.g., pets, religion).

4. Explain that they can move the words and phrases around until they are satisfied that the order reflects their priorities most of the time. Remind them that we all make decisions based on our priorities and our values.

Keeping Mindfulness in Mind

Mindfulness (discussed in Chapters 3 and 4) is about being "in the present." When we ask our students to make decisions—which we do every single day—we want them to be in the present, which requires self-regulation and detachment from situations that could cause stress. Conscious decision making requires an "open" mind, one that is free of stress owing to its ability to handle strong feelings and see others' perspectives (Armstrong, 2019).

Mindfulness has been shown to help with early identification of decisions that have to be made, creative problem solving, thorough ethical evaluation, the ability to recognize the limits of knowledge and therefore limit or extend the search for evidence, and the capacity to identify unintended consequences of possible decisions (Reb & Atkins, 2017). Although the research by Reb and Atkins focuses on decision making in organizations, it has implications for decision making in multiple contexts. For instance, mindfulness allows decision makers to accept feedback and see others' points of view, which can provide more information and thus lead to better decisions for everyone.

In *The Body Keeps the Score*, van der Kolk (2014) refers to mindfulness as the ability "to hover calmly and objectively over our thoughts, feelings, and emotions… and then take our time to respond," which "allows the executive brain to inhibit, organize, and modulate the hardwired automatic reactions preprogrammed into the emotional brain" (p. 62). This allows the brain to be open to multiple options and to make better choices.

Strategies for Decision Making

Because decision making is embedded in every element of teaching and learning, having an array of effective strategies is essential. The following strategies are among those I have gathered from various classrooms, teachers, and schools.

Guts Versus Heads

This idea, from Quist and Gregory (2019), helps teach students the difference between slow and fast thinking. Ask your students to think of a decision that they can make as a class, such as where to go on a field trip at the end of the school year or what should be served each day in the cafeteria. Tell students to use their guts (their first idea or knee-jerk reaction) to quickly come up with their answers (quick thinking). Write these on the board and ask students to think about what matters to them in terms of these choices (here's where values enter the picture). Then ask them to think about each alternative and whether it would do a good job of achieving their objectives (slow thinking). Finally, encourage the students to ask one another questions such as these: *What is it about that alternative that you like? Why did you choose a different alternative than I did?* This activity helps students learn the value of analytical decision making as well as how to listen thoughtfully and empathically to their classmates. Finally, point out the difference between answering with their guts and with their heads. Are they happy with the final decision?

Five-Part Decision Making: The Birthday Party Dilemma

I shared in Chapter 5 that my granddaughter Emmie wasn't invited to a birthday party and was devastated. As her grandmother, I was heartbroken, and I was angry that the invitations had been handed out at school. I used this personal scenario as the basis for the following five-part activity with students.

1. **Identify:** Ask students to determine what the problem is. Give them time to discuss and narrow down the problem to be solved.

2. **Analyze:** Ask students to break down the problem into its parts. What is at the root of the problem?

3. **Brainstorm:** Ask students to come up with possible solutions to this problem. (It's interesting how some kids want to invite all classmates, whereas others just want to find a way to ensure that those who are excluded don't find out!)

4. **Evaluate the solutions:** Create an if/then chart for each suggested solution.

5. **Reflect:** Reflect on the entire process and determine whether the results match your initial target. It's important to take this time to reflect on the decision you made and its outcome. For example, I had one class create a study in which we tried out two solutions to the birthday party invitation dilemma. Shelly had her little sister pass out invitations at school by putting them in individual lockers. The results: those invited made a huge deal of finding the envelope in their lockers.

The jig was up! Andrew had his brother mail invitations to the homes of the students who were invited. Fewer noninvited kids found out about the party, and those who did heard about it after it had occurred. So the students got to discuss which idea worked better and reflect on the results: *Which solution was kinder? Would I do it the same way?* In the end, they decided to discourage birthday parties altogether!

Most kids can relate to this birthday party invitation dilemma; however, keep in mind that some students may have never had a party or gone to one. You know your students. Be thoughtful when choosing a scenario for this five-step decision-making activity.

Offering Choice Through Classroom Jobs

Every day, students are taught lessons that have been carefully crafted by their teacher and are based on a curriculum that follows the state learning standards. In many classes, the classroom walls are covered with rules, goals, and posters chosen by the teacher. The students wear clothing that conforms to the dress code, and they arrive and leave at the times set by the school board and administration. This is not to say that these situations are wrong or unfair, but if we want our students to be good decision makers, they need to have their voices heard and considered when choices are being made that affect them.

One way you can offer more choice is through classroom jobs, which are also a good way to develop decision-making skills. With your class, you can brainstorm answers to the following questions: *What jobs are available? What job would you like to do most? How would you prioritize the jobs according to your favorites or their importance to the classroom?* You can create a "choice board" listing the jobs that you and your students develop, with a description of each job. The list can include anything from "paper-passer-outer" to "phone-picker-upper"! Assign jobs for a week, and if your job list is short, make job sharing an option. Jobs can teach students about shared responsibility, respect (both self-respect and respect for others), and self-management, as well as decision making. On that last point, I had a paper-passer-outer in a 4th grade classroom who had a barrage of questions: *Where do I start—at the back or the front? Do I hand each person their paper, or should they pass them out to the students at their table? Should I stand up to get the papers as soon as you start talking about them, or should I wait until you ask me to do it?* Obviously, the questions revealed some anticipatory anxiety and a lot about how seriously the student took his job! With this in mind, you may want to write protocols for each job and post them.

Debate

An effective way to give students voice and develop their decision-making skills is through debate. The brain likes to be right, and debate is a great way to engage students in conversation with the goal of effectively making a point. You can use a variety of strategies to get students debating, many of which can be used at multiple grade levels. Here are some suggestions.

Traverse Talk. This debate structure, demonstrated in a video on *Edutopia* (2019a), is a great introduction to debate in that it helps students look directly at another person and give opinions. Students stand in parallel lines directly opposite each other. (Standing is preferable to sitting as students can observe body language, maintain eye contact, and generally observe one person at a time.) The teacher gives a provocative "talking point" (an example in the video is "People in wheelchairs can't participate in sports"), either verbally or projected on a screen. After 60 seconds, the students move down the line to debate another talking point with a different classmate.

Four Corners. The Four Corners strategy, which has been used successfully for years, acknowledges student voice, reinforces listening skills, and encourages respectful cooperation. After deciding on a topic, assign a different position on that topic to each corner of the room. Students then choose to stand in the corner that best reflects their personal opinion. Give the students five minutes to work together to create a discussion platform that supports their position. You can provide time and resources for students to gather evidence before the debate begins. Each team presents its opening argument, followed by time for presenting evidence and rebuttals; finally, each team delivers its closing arguments.

SPAR Debates. SPAR is short for *spontaneous argumentation* debates. The term connotes, too, some of the jousting and practicing that we think of as "sparring." SPAR debates can be used with minimal research, so this is a good format for getting students up and debating. It also gives them voice and choice if you allow them to choose their side of the argument.

The following is a simple format to begin "sparring" a debatable issue. In this example, the debate is organized around the question "Would you rather be a postcard or a text message?"

1. Place students in groups of six or eight. Ask half of the group to support one position and the other half to support the other position. Have students move their desks so they are sitting opposite an opponent.

2. Give students one to two minutes to write down their opinion, with evidence for their position.

3. Provide each side with an opportunity to talk together to add to their evidence. This step will help weaker students be prepared to comment.

4. The students will be "sparring" with the person sitting across from them. Each student presents a one-minute opening statement making their case while the opponent listens quietly and takes notes.

5. Give students 30 seconds to prepare ideas for what they want to say to their opponent. Then invite the pairs to engage in

a three-minute discussion during which they may question their opponent's reasoning or examples or put forth new ones of their own.

6. Provide one minute for students to prepare their closing statements. After each student gives a one-minute close, the sparring is over.

7. Take time to debrief. Discuss what students found to be the hardest part. (Listening quietly? Taking notes?) Ask them what value they found in the debate.

Constructive Controversy

You might begin this activity with a discussion of constructive and destructive controversy. This strategy builds on debate and group discussion and follows your class values and norms. One common approach is to assign a cooperative group goal (e.g., passing a test or writing a report). Each group splits into subgroups, which take sides on a given topic and research their respective positions to develop a persuasive argument. The subgroups spend time presenting their argument and refuting the opposition. Finally, the subgroups must take the opposite position, resulting in a synthesis of both positions that represents students' best reasoned judgment.

Magic 8-Ball

This discussion strategy comes from the Ecological Approaches to Social Emotional Learning Laboratory (EASEL) at Harvard University. It is one of many activities the lab calls "kernels," developed to help teachers use SEL (Prothero, 2019). Beneficial for all grade levels, Magic 8-Ball helps students build problem-solving skills.

To begin, the teacher asks, "If a person does X [e.g., crosses the street without looking both ways], what might happen?" Students then "look" inside their imaginary Magic 8-Balls and share their ideas about potential consequences of the action (for example,

"Outlook not so good"). The teacher could then ask how appropriate this response would be in other situations, such as whether to speak while the teacher is speaking. The teacher can follow up by asking students if they see the consequences discussed as positive, negative, or neutral, and in what other situations they might need to imagine an outcome. If the Magic 8-Ball responds with "Better not tell you now," what do you do next?

Dear Abby

Another strategy from the EASEL Lab (Prothero, 2019), Dear Abby is intended to help students explore making responsible, ethical, healthy choices in difficult situations. Although it was designed for 5th grade, it could be applied at any level. First, explain that "Dear Abby" was a newspaper column written by a woman who helped solve people's problems by telling them what she thought of the situation and what they should do. Then use a dilemma from an actual Dear Abby column (or a similar advice column) and ask students to discuss solutions in small groups or to role-play what different dilemmas and their solutions might look like. (Provide any additional information the students might need to better understand the dilemma.) Ask how they think other characters in the scenario would see the situation.

Conver-stations

This discussion strategy keeps students moving and conversations interesting (Gonzalez, 2015). Conver-stations (or conversation stations) can be used with all grade levels and any content area. The steps are as follows:

1. Discuss the class values and norms of behavior.
2. Put students in groups of four to six. Provide them with a question, a statement, or even a name.

3. When students have been conversing for several minutes, have one or two from each group rotate to a different group, while the other group members remain where they are.

4. Remind students to take notes on important points (a task that requires them to choose what to jot down).

5. Once in their new group, students discuss a different but related question, and they may also share some of the key points from their last group's conversation.

6. For the next rotation, students who have not rotated before may move.

This strategy keeps the classroom active, as groups are constantly changing. Because not every student moves at the same time, students have to decide what information is important to take with them to the next group and what to share. Students practice collaborating, being respectful of others, and listening carefully.

Phone a Friend

Some students find decision making very difficult. When game shows started offering contestants the option to ask for help, the phrase "Do you want to phone a friend?" was added to many conversations, sometimes humorously. But the fact is, some decisions do require more information, and letting your students know that they have this option can relieve some stress. Whether this option is offered during assessment time is totally your call (no pun intended). I like to use it for discussions, reading texts and looking for important points, and decision making. In most cases, no actual phone call is made. Instead, the expression simply means you can ask someone for assistance—usually a fellow student. I have also seen teachers allow a phone call to a parent or caregiver, or a visit to another teacher.

Ask Your Audience

Using the same idea as Phone a Friend, but with a slightly different purpose, the Ask Your Audience strategy lets students ask the entire class, their teammates, or even the teacher for help when ideas are not flowing easily. One writing activity I have used for years involves getting input from the class or small groups. To model the process of writing (and because it was fun to do), I generally would write at the same time as my students. I knew that providing a prompt such as "Write about a time when you were very uncomfortable" would lead to students writing about everything from sleeping in a lumpy bed to seeing their parents kissing, so I wrote my first paragraph ahead of time, to share before the others got started. It went like this:

> I was so excited to go on this trip to visit friends in Missouri. We packed up the kids and the dog and made the seven-hour drive to the "motel" where we were staying for a week. The minute we arrived, my heart sank. The motel consisted of some shabby, unpainted cabins with few windows and lots of dirt! I put on my happy face for the kids, and I got straight to work bringing in our things and straightening up. I told myself it would be fine. We spent the day outside. That night I got the kids tucked into their beds, and we headed to ours as we were exhausted from driving and cleaning. As I sat up in bed reading, I felt something crawling on my leg. I jumped out of bed, threw back the covers and found an army of ants! But that wasn't the worst of it.

I stop there. The students' hands are waving frantically in the air. "I would like you to write down three questions that you think the rest of my paper should answer," I tell them. "What would you, the reader, want to know?" Then I say, "I want all of you to begin your stories and read the beginning sentences to the class. We will all provide feedback for you. This is a wonderful way to get to know your audience."

A General Guide to Decision Making in Your Class

The following guide outlines the many ways in which decision making plays a role in your classroom instruction. It is applicable to any grade level.

- Within a topic, focus on decisions related to specific content. For example, if you are studying the pioneers of 1840 traveling west, the discussion could focus on pioneers' decisions on what to leave behind and what to take with them.
- Decide on the question, problem, or situation that will have to be addressed by you or your students. If you are studying gravity, you may have students decide on the importance of Sir Isaac Newton's contribution compared with Albert Einstein's.
- Decide if you want to put your students in the role of decision makers or evaluators of decisions already made. For example, in a literature study of *Romeo and Juliet,* ask students to list the characters' decisions and then evaluate whether the decisions were good or bad. What would they suggest the characters do differently?
- Decide which sources students will use to gather information. You and your students can decide together what textbooks, interviews, or Internet sources will be most helpful.
- Decide on the best method for problem solving. In math, for example, students can try different mathematical approaches for solving a problem and then determine which method is the easiest, the shortest, or the most practical.
- Decide on the criteria to be used to compare and contrast alternatives (unless you want students to do this themselves as part of the process). This can begin with a project in any content area. It may be best to have the group brainstorm the criteria. For example, when I ask students to compare and

contrast Hershey's Hugs and Kisses, will they base their decisions on visual appeal, taste, texture, or ingredients? When various groups or teams in your class are comparing their findings, they must all be using the same criteria.

• Decide how students can best communicate their decisions. What platform would be best for both sharing and evaluating decisions, keeping in mind the intended audience? Students may be able to choose what platform they are most comfortable with, and you can limit these choices by providing a list that includes options such as PowerPoint presentations, Prezis, skits or role-plays, commercials, or written documents.

Every Student Has a Story

Some of our students have never been allowed to make a decision, whereas others have been punished or ignored because of their choices. It is important that we teach students that they can make mistakes. Failure is an option. You may have to remind them that you believe—and they should also believe—that their brains can change, and they have the ability to achieve. Consider the following if/then situations.

If...	Then...
A student is afraid of making choices because of past experiences,	Begin an activity with a short discussion about growth mindset and our ability to change our brain.

If...	Then...
Students become intent on being "right" without evidence to support their stance,	Remind them of their social contract or class values and norms. Ask them to do the research or to be willing to accept the research others are using to prove their point.
A student uses his gut feelings and knows he is right,	Tell him to follow his feelings and find the proof necessary for others to agree with him.
A student does not agree with the group decision,	Ask her to examine the evidence that the group has gathered and try to find irrefutable proof that the group is wrong. (Remind the student that this is a great way to build new connections in the brain.)
A debate becomes a shouting match with statements like "No! You are wrong,"	Provide sentence starters, such as "I agree because _____" and "I strongly disagree, but I respect your right to believe that." As a class, create your own sentence starters based on your class values.

8

People, Not Programs: The Positive Impact of SEL

In the past jobs were about muscles, now they're about brains, but in future they'll be about the heart.

—Minouche Shafik

Five parents entered the conference room and sat down with the superintendent of schools. Mr. Whitaker almost never met with parents over classroom issues; that was the principal's job, and even then only when the teacher had exhausted all efforts to deal with the situation. The particular school these parents represented was a K–8 building with a strong principal who was raising test scores in her own inimitable way. Even Mr. Whitaker knew that you didn't mess with Dr. Jo Anne Burns. She was a force.

Curiosity persuaded Mr. Whitaker to meet with the parents. If they were going over Dr. Burns's head, they'd better have a good reason. They did. The parents' appointed spokesperson, Andy

Fox, began: "We have an issue at Hanes Elementary. Our 4th graders are afraid to go to school, and they come home angry or tearful. We think it's because of their language arts teacher, Mrs. Fisher. She's a bully."

At this, Lana Hulick chimed in: "That teacher is relentless. She pushes and pushes them to do well for the state test. It's as though learning itself doesn't even matter to her. My daughter comes home and tells me how the students who aren't doing well get yelled at!"

"And humiliated," added Carol Brooks, another parent at the table.

Andy said, "When I asked Mrs. Fisher why my son feels picked on, she said he couldn't sit still or focus, and she had to constantly remind him what he should be doing. After each of us had parent conferences with Mrs. Fisher, we concluded that she wasn't going to change. So we went to Dr. Burns. She backed up the teacher, and then she reiterated the importance of raising test scores. She also said that my kid has an attention problem! So I took him over to MSU and had him tested. No attention problem. Do I have to homeschool my child to lower his stress? He's always been happy at school!"

Carol asked, "Seriously, Mr. Whitaker, what is going on here? Are the teachers getting more pressure about test scores from the principal? Is this a case where the principal is bullying the teachers and then they bully the kids?"

It's well established that people who bully have often been bullied themselves (Haltigan & Vaillancourt, 2014). Although we wish that bullies would eventually get their comeuppance, it usually doesn't happen that way. Rather than bullies becoming victims, victims become bullies.

What happens inside the heads of people who are bullied? The fight-or-flight response kicks in, cortisol is released, and the brain can focus only on the threat at hand. If Mrs. Fisher's students were having problems focusing in her class and not in others, then the situation was being created in her classroom.

This happens to most teachers, at least on a smaller scale. My principal once came in to see me and mentioned that I was the only teacher sending a particular student to the office; he had no problems in any other classroom. The message was clear: *Marilee Sprenger has an issue with a student and needs to deal with it.* Given this information, I reframed my interactions with this student. My assumption that he had it in for me was irrational; he was merely trying to survive in my class. I figured out how to help him do so, and it saved us both from the stress we'd been having over the issue.

Mr. Whitaker said he would look into the problem at Hanes Elementary. Although the parents left the meeting unsure that anything would change, they were pleasantly surprised by the result. Mr. Whitaker found that the issue was indeed a trickle-down effect: Mrs. Fisher was completely stressed out about test scores because Dr. Burns was putting so much pressure on the teachers to raise them. To everyone's credit, the school and the classroom climate improved. It didn't happen overnight, but knowing that the powers that be were exerting effort, the parents were able to assure their kids that things were going to get better.

Student Regulation Begins with Adult Regulation

Teachers need to address their own stress before they can help students with stress management. In Chapter 4, I addressed the three types of stress: positive stress, tolerable stress, and toxic stress.

According to Burns (2019), teachers experience tolerable stress all day at school as they manage the classroom. But most often teachers go home and destress themselves by interacting with their families or friends, working on a project that is not school related, or relaxing with a good book or other favorite activity. Whatever they choose, most educators can destress.

But when teachers are stressed because they themselves are being bullied, what then? Who's doing the bullying? Students may bully teachers with their behavior, always pushing the envelope. It becomes a challenge for teachers trying to understand and provide a safe environment if some of the students are acting out, spreading rumors, or cyberbullying them. Parents can be bullies, too. Some hover around and get pushy about what they want for their child. Some may be Facebook "friends" with teachers or have teachers' e-mail addresses, and they may use these platforms to make demands that sound like threats or feel like harassment. Principals can also bully teachers. Under pressure for delivering high test scores, they may have some impossible expectations and blame teachers for outcomes that are lower than hoped for. One teacher told me her treatment by the principal was determined by test scores. If her students did well, she was treated like a star, but if they fell short, the principal ignored her or was rude.

Teacher stress can be overwhelming. Mrs. Fisher, the teacher in this chapter's opening anecdote, was a hardworking, caring teacher under ordinary circumstances. Testing often puts a strain on administrators, teachers, and students. As the cheerleading coach at one school, I was once told to create a pep assembly for the state test. I was shocked that I had to train my cheerleaders, change the wording of our cheers, and coordinate with other teachers, all to encourage our students to do well on the test! It wasn't a terrible idea, but it stressed the test, which stressed the students and the teachers. We know now that through better teaching strategies—including those that incorporate the five components of SEL—students will learn more and retain what they need for the future.

Addressing teacher stress is crucial for creating the culture and climate necessary to obtain the highest gains from implementing SEL. Students walk into our schools carrying their loads of stress, and some teachers go home carrying theirs.

Three Terms to Know

Secondary traumatic stress (STS), compassion fatigue, and *decision fatigue* are real conditions that can cause teacher burnout and a desire to leave the job. What characterizes these conditions, and what can we do about them?

Secondary traumatic stress has been defined by the National Child Traumatic Stress Network (NCTSN) as "the emotional duress that results when an individual hears about the firsthand trauma experiences of another." Listening to and working with students who have experienced or are experiencing trauma can cause educators to experience this "secondhand" trauma. Cognitive behavioral strategies and mindfulness have been shown to help deal with this stress (NCTSN, 2019).

Compassion fatigue is somewhat synonymous with STS. It is sometimes referred to as "burnout," but burnout is more serious than compassion fatigue. Before reaching the point of burnout, individuals can do several things to remedy the situation. Because many of those affected are in a helping or healing profession, it is useful for them to "unload" some of the fatigue they feel by journaling, meditating, exercising, doing more things outside work, and reaching out to others. Neuroscientist Matthew Lieberman (2019) says that burnout is contagious, and we need to help others before they get to that point. One of his suggestions is for teachers to have common break times (free periods) during which they can get to know one another better, build community, and talk things out.

Decision fatigue is something that can happen to anyone, including students. Have you ever gone home after school and responded to a family member who asks what's for dinner by saying, "I don't want to make one more decision today—my brain is fried!"? In its simplest form, decision fatigue comes from making too many decisions, which has always made me wonder if the classes at the end of the day seemed more difficult because I just didn't want to make another decision. Roy Baumeister coined the term *decision fatigue*, and in his book about willpower, he says that making decisions requires the same willpower as turning down a donut (Gamb, 2019). Former president Barack Obama told *Vanity Fair* (Lewis, 2012) that he wore only gray or blue suits to pare down the decisions he had to make.

Recall that teachers make about 1,500 educational decisions each day (Goldberg & Houser, 2017). To avoid decision fatigue, some have suggested that we make all our decisions in the morning—but that strategy works only for those who teach morning kindergarten! Educators need to take weekends off (no grading papers or designing new lessons), simplify meals by stocking up on healthy snacks and preplanning menus, and decide what they're going to wear the night before. By creating simple, predictable morning routines—including everything from planning what they'll eat for breakfast to allotting 10 minutes for exercise or meditation—teachers can put their brains on automatic and save their mental energy for solving more challenging problems later in the day.

A study of judicial decision making (Danziger, Levav, & Avnaim-Pesso, 2011) suggested that judges don't base their decisions on the law alone. The study, conducted to determine the basis on which judges decided whether a prisoner would get paroled, found that the decision depended on the time of day the case came before them:

later in the day, the judges made less favorable rulings. Educators, too, are making decisions or "judgments" throughout the day. When they don't have time to themselves—prep periods, planning time, or mental breaks—those judgments will likely increase in harshness.

How Emotions Affect Decision Making

Sometimes, teaching middle school ELA involves grading a lot of papers in a short time. So it was one Thursday night that I had essays from three classes to grade. I had provided a rubric that the students had stapled to one side of their papers, with the writing prompt on the other. The intent was to help the students check the rubric and their paper while writing, and it helped me too, as I could score the essay using the rubric that was handily attached.

By 10:30 p.m., I was exhausted. My head was spinning and my eyes were blurry as I read yet another compare/contrast essay on two characters from a story we had been reading and dis-cussing. I took the final paper out of my briefcase. It was Josh's paper. Josh's face flashed before my eyes, and several incidents and encounters with him spilled from my memory. He was not a student who put forth much effort, and I had little expectation that he would show any in this paper, but I hoped I was wrong. I read the paper, filled out the rubric, wrote several comments, added up his score, and wrote his grade on the rubric. Done! I sighed with relief, gathered the papers, and stuffed all 75 into my case.

The next morning brought sunshine and hope for a good weekend. My students were expecting me to return their papers. When the first-hour students arrived in the classroom, I took out their papers and began passing them out. When I got to Josh's paper, I saw that the cover paper—the rubric with his grade—was not attached. I thought it might have been torn off when I put the papers back in my case. I searched but could not find it.

When Josh shouted, "Mrs. S., I didn't get my paper back!" I called him over. "Josh, I am still considering your grade. It was late last night, and I want to be sure I gave your paper my complete attention. I will get it back to you by the end of class."

OK, crisis averted. While the class was doing their silent reading, I grabbed another rubric and began reading Josh's paper for the second (or third) time. I filled out the rubric, made comments to acknowledge his strengths, and asked questions to guide him in improving his writing. I completed the process and wrote a *B* on the top of the rubric. At the end of class, I told Josh what I liked about the paper and sent him off happily to his next class. At the end of the day, I packed up my briefcase with more papers for the weekend. As I started to close the top, I noticed a piece of paper peeking out from between two dividers. It was Josh's rubric from last night. I had done extra work (rereading his essay) because of my carelessness. As I read over the rubric and comments from the previous evening, however, embarrassment washed over me. Last night, Josh's grade had been a *C*; today it was a *B!*

Although we believe we are objective when it comes to grading, our mood, our emotions, and our prior encounters with students—and even the number of decisions we've already made—can creep in and affect the grades we give. This is true even when we use a rubric. I'm living (although dying of embarrassment) proof! And there's more.

In a study conducted at Yale University (Brackett, 2019), teachers were divided into two groups. One group was asked to think about their positive classroom experiences, and the other was told to focus on a negative experience. Then all the participants were asked to grade the same middle school paper. The results? Those who were thinking positively graded the paper a full grade higher than those who had recalled the negative experience. The teachers did not believe that their emotions affected the grading; however, the research disproved their belief.

From ACEs to PACEs

As explained earlier, the acronym *ACEs* refers to adverse childhood experiences. These include abuse, abandonment, an incarcerated family member, alcoholism, death, divorce, mental illness, and poverty, among others. What many people refer to as *counter-ACEs* include close friends, close neighbors, comforting beliefs, a positive regard for school, caring teachers, a trusted caregiver, a feeling of safety, fun, and a predictable home routine. I like to use a term used by author and neuroscientist Martha Burns (2019) of Northwest University: *PACEs* (positive advantageous childhood experiences).

Current research from Brigham Young University (BYU) (2019) indicates how vital it is that kids have positive childhood experiences. Studies during the last 20 years or so, including a landmark study sponsored by the Centers for Disease Control and Prevention and Kaiser Permanente (Felitti et al., 1998), had concluded that having four or more ACEs increased negative health outcomes later in life, including depression, higher body mass index, and higher rates of smoking. However, according to BYU assistant professor of public health Ali Crandall and her coauthors (2019), positive experiences can potentially negate or reverse the harmful health effects of ACEs: "If your child has experienced trauma and you're worried about the long-term impact it could have on them, these findings show that the positive experiences in childhood lead to better adult physical and mental health, no matter what they have faced." The BYU researchers reported that even if someone had four or more ACEs, a high number of advantageous experiences could lessen the negative health effects later in life. (Among the study participants, nearly three-fourths had had at least one ACE, and the average number was 2.67. The average number of counter-ACEs was 8.15.)

Conversely, the study results also revealed the damaging effects of having *no* positive experiences. After looking at the physical health of the participants (using factors including exercise, sleep habits, smoking, and diet) and their mental health and cognitive abilities (using factors such as executive-functioning abilities, levels of stress, depression, and ability to deal with challenging situations), the researchers discovered that the absence of positive experiences led to poor adult health no matter how many ACEs the individual had. As Crandall and colleagues noted, "As bad as ACEs may be, the absence of these positive childhood experiences and relationships may actually be more detrimental to lifelong health, so we need more focus on increasing the positive."

Although a child's family situation accounted for many of the adverse childhood experiences in this study, Crandall and colleagues noted the importance of "other adults in a child's life that are not the parent, like extended family, teachers, neighbors, friends and youth leaders." These, they said, "all help to increase the number of counter-ACEs and boost lifelong health."

The message for educators is clear: we can make a major difference in the present and future quality of life for our students. The topics covered in this book—including such things as building relationships and teaching empathy so students can better understand the actions and viewpoints of others—are ways that educators can create positive experiences in the classroom. Working on all the SEL competencies as delineated by CASEL and presented in the introduction to this book (self-awareness, self-management, social awareness, relationship skills, and responsible decision making) will help students feel that they belong and they are safe.

CASEL held an SEL Exchange in October 2019 in which current and former leaders from the original districts that have collaborated and implemented SEL since 2011 met to discuss what they would change. The one insight they all shared was that they wished they had focused more on the adults. Teachers, they agreed, need to feel valued and empowered in order to carry out the important task of teaching SEL to students and embedding SEL into their classes each day.

Getting to Know Every Child

An article titled "The Power of Being Seen" (Korbey, 2017) tells the powerful story of how Cold Springs Middle School in Nevada turned itself around by getting to know students through an effort that involved *every* teacher and *every* student. The Washoe County School District, which Cold Springs is part of, began an SEL program in 2012, and it has since seen improvements such as higher attendance, higher test scores, higher graduation rates, and better mental health.

The district's mission statement is "Every Child, by Name and Face, to Graduation." One way Cold Springs worked on this mission was to use a strategy it calls a "teacher/student connection activity." All teachers (I would add all staff) gathered in a room in which posters hanging on the wall listed every student's name. Next to the names were columns with the headings "Name/Face," "Something Personal," "Personal/Family Story," and "Academic Standing." Teachers used markers to make checkmarks in the columns if they knew information in that category. As they gathered around different posters, they shared information about the students they knew and asked questions about those they didn't. They engaged in personal reflections after this process and began connecting more with students between classes or at other available times. Their effort led to a community in which students felt seen and cared for.

Every Student Has a Story— and Every Educator Has a Responsibility

It is critical that all stakeholders—including boards of education, parents, administrators, and teachers—understand the necessity and the promise of social-emotional learning. Recognizing the importance of SEL and understanding how the brain develops and learns can provide the background knowledge necessary to realize that every student's success relies on all of us modeling, teaching, encouraging, and providing opportunities to build healthier systems of support in all our schools.

We can't simply *think* we are teaching SEL ("Oh, yes, we have an SEL program; the students meet with a person on Friday for 30 minutes to do SEL lessons"); we must incorporate it into everything we do at school. Everyone should be practicing SEL with their students every day, in every way.

Furthermore, SEL needs to be trauma-aware. If we are going to create an environment where all individuals—teachers and students alike—can trust one another and feel secure in the knowledge that they are part of a caring community, then we need to work on support for all. Together we can create a culture of friendship, strong working relationships, and a safe place for dealing with emotion. We may have to emphasize routines and rituals more for students with ACEs. We may need to slow down the curriculum for students who are just becoming more able to use their cognitive skills because their brains have been bound up by emotion that they could never handle before. It may take some extra effort to counterbalance ACEs with PACEs, but SEL can have a positive impact, especially when using a neuroscience-based approach. As a colleague asked me, "Do we want our schools to be pain-based or brain-based?"

In the introduction, I shared that according to psychiatrist Bruce Perry, *people,* not programs, change people (Perry & Szalavitz, 2007). You and I—*we* are those people.

The following if/then table suggests resources you can turn to for more information.

If...	Then...
You want more information on restorative justice,	Check out *Hacking School Discipline* by Nathan Maynard and Brad Weinstein, or *Better Than Carrots or Sticks* by Dominique Smith, Douglas Fisher, and Nancy Frey.
You want to delve more deeply into the brain and trauma,	Read Nadine Burke Harris's *The Deepest Well,* or Bessel van der Kolk's *The Body Keeps the Score.*
You would like more information about the social-emotional learning competencies,	Visit http://CASEL.org.
You would like to look more deeply at empathy,	Read *End Peer Cruelty, Build Empathy* or *UnSelfie* by Michele Borba, or *Roots of Empathy* by Mary Gordon.
You are interested in learning more about how to teach your students about their brains,	Read *The Whole-Brain Child* by Daniel J. Siegel and Tina Payne Bryson, or find Siegel's videos on YouTube.

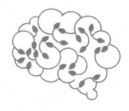

Glossary

Amygdala: An almond-shaped structure found in each hemisphere of the brain. Part of the limbic system, the amygdala is associated with emotional memory and emotional responses.

Anterior cingulate: A midbrain structure known to coordinate emotions and thinking.

Anterior insula: A small region in the cerebral cortex that relays messages associated with social engagement, empathy, and emotions.

Brain stem: This posterior brain region, located at the base of the brain, controls the flow of messages between the brain and the body. This vital structure is the part of the brain that is associated with instincts and controls the body's vital functions, such as heart rate, breathing, body temperature, and balance.

Cerebellum: A structure in the back and bottom of the brain; sometimes called "the little brain." It has many functions, including aiding in the interpretation of socially relevant signals to understand intentions as well as the mental and emotional states of others.

Cortisol: The primary stress-related hormone, crucial in preparing the body for the fight-or-flight response.

Dopamine: The "feel-good" neurotransmitter that is released when, for example, individuals find friendship and seek goals.

Dorsolateral prefrontal cortex: An area of the brain that is typically associated with executive functions such as working memory and decision making.

Endorphins: Neurotransmitters that are the brain's opioids and are released in response to physical pain and to help relieve stress.

Hippocampus: The structure, next to the amygdala, that aids in memory storage.

Homeostasis: A state of internal balance and stability among interdependent elements.

Inferior parietal lobe: A part of the parietal lobe that is involved in the perception of emotions.

Insula: A structure in the cerebral cortex that plays a significant role in emotions, empathy, and social engagement.

Limbic system: The area of the brain associated with emotions, encompassing the amygdala, the hippocampus, and the hypothalamus, along with other smaller structures.

Mammalian brain: A term referring to the limbic system.

Medial prefrontal cortex: A part of the prefrontal cortex that is involved in one's sense of self, or self-awareness.

Mirror neurons: Brain cells that fire when a person does something and watches someone else do the same thing. They "mirror" what is happening and are believed to also mirror emotions.

Noradrenaline: A neurotransmitter, also known as norepinephrine, that prepares the body for action and is vital to the fight-or-flight response.

Nucleus accumbens: A small structure in the limbic system that provides rewards by releasing dopamine into the prefrontal cortex.

Orbital prefrontal cortex: A part of the prefrontal cortex, located behind the eyes, that is critical to self-awareness.

Oxytocin: A neurotransmitter, sometimes called the "cuddle chemical," that is released when feeling connected or bonded to another.

Posterior cingulate: A midline region at the back of the brain that provides a sense of one's physical location.

Prefrontal cortex: The part of the frontal lobe that is in charge of executive functions, impulse control, and decision making. It can temper the amygdala and evaluate emotional situations.

Reticular activating system: The brain's first filter for incoming information, located in the brain stem. It decides what information is to be sent to the prefrontal cortex and what is to be ignored.

Right supramarginal gyrus: Part of the parietal lobe that is heavily responsible for the ability to put aside egocentricity and empathize with others.

Serotonin: A brain chemical that contributes to well-being and happiness, released when a person feels good about social status or receives positive feedback on accomplishments. It is involved in learning and memory.

Superior temporal sulcus: A structure located in the temporal lobe, implicated in recognizing the purpose of an interaction and one's social awareness.

Temporoparietal junction: An area where the temporal and parietal lobes meet, involved with the superior temporal sulcus in social awareness and social interaction.

Ventrolateral prefrontal cortex: An area in the prefrontal cortex that is responsible for goal-appropriate responses in relation to decision making.

Ventromedial prefrontal cortex: An area in the prefrontal cortex that processes risk as it relates to decision making.

References

Allday, R. A., Bush, M., Ticknor, N., & Walker, L. (2011). Using teacher greetings to increase speed to task engagement. *Journal of Applied Behavior Analysis, 44*(2), 393–396.

Allday, R. A., & Pakurar, K. (2007). Effects of teacher greetings on student on-task behavior. *Journal of Applied Behavior Analysis 40*(2), 317–320.

Alliance of Therapy Dogs. (2017). *The benefits of therapy dogs in classrooms and on college campuses*. Retrieved from https://www.therapydogs.com/therapy-dogs-classrooms-campuses/

Armstrong, T. (2016). *The power of the adolescent brain: Strategies for teaching middle and high school students*. Alexandria, VA: ASCD.

Armstrong, T. (2019). *Mindfulness in the classroom: Strategies for promoting concentration, compassion, and calm*. Alexandria, VA: ASCD.

Aronson, E. (2000). *The jigsaw classroom*. Social Psychology Network. Retrieved from http://www.jigsaw.org/

Barrett, L. F. (2018). *How emotions are made: The secret life of the brain*. New York: Mariner Books.

Beach, M. (2010, May). Creating empathy in the classroom. *TEACH Magazine*. Retrieved from https://teachmag.com/archives/1115

Beauchesne, K. (2018). 24 awesome ways to encourage being kind at school. *PTO Today*. Retrieved from https://www.ptotoday.com/pto-today-articles/article/8862-awesome-ways-to-encourage-being-kind-at-school

Beck, A. E. (1994). On universities: J. Tuzo Wilson Medal acceptance speech. *Elements: Newsletter of the Canadian Geophysical Union, 12,* 7–9.

Bland, K. (2018). Blue eyes, brown eyes: What Jane Elliott's famous experiment says about race 50 years on. *The Republic.* Retrieved from https://www.azcentral.com/story/news/local/karinabland/2017/11/17/blue-eyes-brown-eyes-jane-elliotts-exercise-race-50-years-later/860287001/

Bloom, B. S., Engelhart, M. D., Furst, E. J., Hill, W. H., & Krathwohl, D. R. (Eds.). (1956). *Taxonomy of educational objectives: The classification of educational goals. Handbook I: Cognitive domain.* New York: David McKay.

Boaler, J. (2019). *Limitless mind: Learn, lead, and live without barriers.* New York: HarperOne.

Bolte Taylor, J. (2006). *My stroke of insight: A brain scientist's personal journey.* New York: Penguin Group.

Borba, M. (2016). *Unselfie: Why empathetic kids succeed in our all-about-me world.* New York: Touchstone.

Brackett, M. (2019). *Permission to feel: Unlocking the power of emotions to help our kids, ourselves, and our society thrive.* New York: Celadon.

Bradley, L. (2017, December 12). Putting empathy and digital citizenship at the center of our classrooms. *KQED Education.* Retrieved from https://ww2.kqed.org/education/2017/12/12/putting-empathy-and-digital-citizenship-at-the-center-of-our-classrooms/

Brigham Young University. (2019, September 16). For kids who face trauma, good neighbors or teachers can save their longterm health. *Science-Daily.* Retrieved from https://www.sciencedaily.com/releases/2019/09/190916144004.htm

Brighten, T. (2017, November 10). Why students should develop their personal brand as they apply to university. *BridgeU.* Retrieved from https://bridge-u.com/blog/help-students-develop-personal-brands/

Brookhart, S. (2017). *How to give effective feedback to your students* (2nd ed.). Alexandria, VA: ASCD.

Brown, B. (2018). *Dare to lead: Brave work. Tough conversations. Whole hearts.* New York: Random House.

Burke Harris, N. (2018). *The deepest well: Healing the long-term effects of childhood adversity.* New York: Houghton Mifflin Harcourt.

Burns, M. (2019, November 23). *The positive student impact of social-emotional learning and neuroscience-based approaches* [Webinar]. Fast ForWord Scientific Learning. Retrieved from https://pages.scilearn.com/Webinar-AOD-MBurns-Positive-Impact-of-SEL.html

Burton, R. (2019). Our brains tell stories so we can live. *Nautilus*. Retrieved from http://nautil.us/issue/75/story/our-brains-tell-stories-so-we-can-live

Camden, T., Dennison, C., Hinnen, N., Leonard, J., Smith, B. L., Taubert, C., et al. (n.d.). *Family tools: Decision-making*. Peoria, IL: Heart of Illinois United Way. Retrieved from https://www.hoiunitedway.org/wp-content/uploads/HOIUW-HMHN-Decision-Making-Skills-Booklet.pdf

Cantor, P. (2019, February 13). *The school of the future: A conversation with Dr. Pamela Cantor* [Presentation]. Turnaround for Children. Retrieved from https://www.turnaroundusa.org/school-of-the-future-gsvlabs/

Carmody, D. P., & Lewis, M. (2006). Brain activation when hearing one's own and others' names. *Brain Research, 1116*(1), 153–158. Retrieved from https://www.sciencedirect.com/science/article/abs/pii/S0006899306022682

CASEL. (2017). *Core SEL competencies*. Chicago: Author. Retrieved from https://casel.org/core-competencies

CASEL. (2019, November). Strengthening adult SEL. *SEL Trends, 7*. Retrieved from https://casel.org/wp-content/uploads/2019/11/SEL-Trends-7-11182019.pdf

Center on the Developing Child. (n.d.). *Toxic stress*. Cambridge, MA: Center on the Developing Child, Harvard University. Retrieved from https://developingchild.harvard.edu/science/key-concepts/toxic-stress/

Centers for Disease Control and Prevention. (n.d.). *Adverse childhood experiences (ACEs): Preventing early trauma to improve adult health*. Atlanta, GA: Author. Retrieved from https://www.cdc.gov/vitalsigns/aces/index.html

Clough, S., & Hilverman, C. (2018). Hand gestures and how they help children learn. *Frontiers for Young Minds, 6*(29).

Coan, J. A., Becks, L., & Hasselmo, K. (2013). Familiarity promotes the blurring of self and other in the neural representation of threat. *Social Cognitive and Affective Neuroscience, 8*(6), 670–677.

Cook, C. R., Coco, S., Zhang, Y., Fiat, A. E., Duong, M. T., Renshaw, T. L., et al. (2018). Cultivating positive teacher-student relationships: Preliminary evaluation of the establish-maintain-restore (EMR) method. *School Psychology Review, 47*(3), 226–243.

Cook, C., Fiat, A., & Larson, M. (2018, February 19). Positive greetings at the door: Evaluation of a low-cost, high-yield proactive classroom management strategy. *Journal of Positive Behavior Interventions, 20*(3), 149–159.

Covey, S. (2015). *The Stephen R. Covey interactive reader—4 books in 1: The 7 habits of highly effective people, first things first, and the best of the most renowned leadership teacher of our time.* Coral Gables, FL: Mango Media.

Crandall, A., Miller, J. R., Cheung, A., Novilla, L. K., Glade, R., Novilla, M. L. B., et al. (2019). ACEs and counter-ACEs: How positive and negative childhood experiences influence adult health. *Child Abuse & Neglect, 96,* 104089.

Danziger, S., Levav, J., & Avnaim-Pesso, L. (2011). Extraneous factors in judicial decisions. *PNAS, 108*(17), 6889–6892.

Darling-Hammond, L. (2019). Demonstrating self-regulation with tone of voice [Video]. *How Learning Happens* series. *Edutopia.* Retrieved from https://www.edutopia.org/video/demonstrating-self-regulation-tone-voice

Darling-Hammond, L., Flook, L., Cook-Harvey, C., Barron, B., & Osher, D. (2019). Implications for educational practice of the science of learning and development. *Journal of Applied Developmental Science, 24*(2), 97–140.

Davis, K. L., & Montag, C. (2019). Selected principles of Pankseppian affective neuroscience. *Frontiers in Neuroscience, 12,* 1025.

Desautels, L., & McKnight, M. (2019). *Eyes are never quiet: Listening beneath the behaviors of our most troubled students.* Deadwood, OR: Wyatt-MacKenzie.

Djikic, M., & Oatley, K. (2014). The art in fiction: From indirect communication to changes of the self. *Psychology of Aesthetics, Creativity, and the Arts, 8*(4), 498–505.

Dunning, D. L., Griffiths, K., Kuyken, W., Crane, C., Foulkes, L., Parker, J., et al. (2019, March). Research review: The effects of mindfulness-based interventions on cognition and mental health in children and adolescents —a meta-analysis of randomized controlled trials. *Journal of Child Psychology and Psychiatry, 60*(3), 244–258.

Durlak, J. A., Weissberg, R. P., Dymnicki, A. B., Taylor, R. D., & Schellinger, K. B. (2011). The impact of enhancing students' social and emotional learning: A meta-analysis of school-based universal interventions. *Child Development, 82,* 405–432.

Dweck, C. (2016, January 13). What having a "growth mindset" actually means. *Harvard Business Review.* Retrieved from https://hbr.org/2016/01/what-having-a-growth-mindset-actually-means

Edutopia. (2014, July 1). Dialogue circles and positive classroom cultures. Retrieved from https://www.edutopia.org/practice/stw-glenview-practice-dialogue-circles-video

Edutopia. (2019a). 60-second strategy: Traverse talk. Retrieved from https://www.edutopia.org/video/60-second-strategy-traverse-talk

Edutopia. (2019b). Social contracts foster community in the classroom. Retrieved from https://www.edutopia.org/video/social-contracts-foster-community-classroom

Elias, M. J., & Tobias, S. E. (2018). *Boost emotional intelligence in students: 30 flexible research-based activities to build EQ skills (grades 5–9).* Minneapolis, MN: Free Spirit Publishing.

Felitti, V. J., Anda, R. F., Nordenberg, D., Williamson, D. F., Spitz, A. M., Edwards, V., et al. (1998). Relationship of childhood abuse and household dysfunction to many of the leading causes of death in adults: The adverse childhood experiences (ACE) study. *American Journal of Preventive Medicine, 14*(4), 245–258.

Files, E. (2019). How assigned seats during lunchtime can foster a positive school culture. *MindShift.* Retrieved from https://www.kqed.org/mindshift/54644/how-assigned-seats-during-lunchtime-can-foster-a-positive-school-culture

Fisher, D., & Frey, N. (2019, May). Show & tell: A video column/"There was this teacher…." *Educational Leadership, 76*(8), 82–83.

Fletcher, J. (2019). 5 ways to incorporate SEL in middle school. *Edutopia.* Retrieved from https://www.edutopia.org/article/5-ways-incorporate-sel-middle-school

Foreman, D. (2019). How to build an effective system for responding to behavioral infractions. *Turnaround for Children. The 180 Blog.* Retrieved from https://www.turnaroundusa.org/how-to-build-an-effective-system-for-responding-to-behavioral-infractions/

Frey, N., Fisher, D., & Smith, D. (2019). *All learning is social and emotional: Helping students develop essential skills for the classroom and beyond.* Alexandria, VA: ASCD.

Gaines, P. (2019, October 11). California's first surgeon general: Screen every student for childhood trauma. *NBC News Learn.* Retrieved from http://www.nbcnews.com/news/nbcblk/california-s-first-surgeon-general-screen-every-student-childhood-trauma-n1064286

Gamb, M. (2019, May 13). How to identify when you're experiencing decision fatigue. *Forbes.* Retrieved from https://www.forbes.com/sites/womensmedia/2019/05/13/how-to-identify-when-youre-experiencing-decision-fatigue/

Goldberg, G., & Houser, R. (2017, July 19). Battling decision fatigue. *Edutopia.* Retrieved from https://www.edutopia.org/blog/battling-decision-fatigue-gravity-goldberg-renee-houser

Goleman, D. (1995). *Emotional intelligence.* New York: Bantam Books.

Gonzalez, J. (2015, October 15). The big list of class discussion strategies [Blog post]. *Cult of Pedagogy.* Retrieved from https://www.cultofpedagogy.com/speaking-listening-techniques/

Gordon, K. (2012). How to teach kids gratitude and empathy. *New York Family*. Retrieved from https://www.newyorkfamily.com/how-to-teach-kids-gratitude-and-empathy/

Gordon, M. (2009). *Roots of empathy: Changing the world child by child.* New York: The Experiment.

Gordon, M. (2010). *Roots and seeds of empathy.* Retrieved from http://cultureofempathy.com/References/Experts/Mary-Gordon.htm

Grate, M. (2014, October 1). Bullyproof your classroom with brown paper bags. *Middleweb*. Retrieved from https://www.middleweb.com/18809/a-strategy-improve-classroom-culture/

Graves, G. (2017). Unlock your emotional intelligence. *The Science of Emotions* (pp. 9–13). New York: Time Books.

Gregoire, C. (2018). How money changes the way you think and feel. *Greater Good Magazine*. Retrieved from https://greatergood.berkeley.edu/article/item/how_money_changes_the_way_you_think_and_feel

Gregory, G., & Kaufeldt, M. (2015). *The motivated brain: Improving student attention, engagement, and perseverance.* Alexandria, VA: ASCD.

Grewal, D. (2012, April 10). How wealth reduces compassion. *Scientific American*. Retrieved from https://www.scientificamerican.com/article/how-wealth-reduces-compassion/

Grove, C., & Henderson, L. (2018, March 19). Therapy dogs can help reduce student stress, anxiety and improve school attendance. *The Conversation*. Retrieved from https://theconversation.com/therapy-dogs-can-help-reduce-student-stress-anxiety-and-improve-school-attendance-93073

Haltigan, J., & Vaillancourt, T. (2014). Joint trajectories of bullying and peer victimization across elementary and middle school and associations with symptoms of psychopathology. *Developmental Psychology, 50*(11), 2426–2436.

Hartwell-Walker, M. (2018, October 8). Click or clique: Positive and negative teen social groups. *PsychCentral*. Retrieved from https://psychcentral.com/lib/click-or-clique-positive-and-negative-teen-social-groups/

Hattie, J. (2012). *Visible learning for teachers: Maximizing impact on learning.* New York: Routledge.

Hattie, J. (2017). Hattie ranking: 252 influences and effect sizes related to student achievement. *Visible Learning*. Retrieved from https://visible-learning.org/hattie-ranking-influences-effect-sizes-learning-achievement/

Hiser, J., & Koenigs, M. (2018). The multifaceted role of ventromedial prefrontal cortex in emotion, decision making, social cognition, and psychopathology. *Biological Psychiatry, 83*(8), 638–647.

Hoffman, M. (1991). *Amazing grace.* New York: Dial Books.

Immordino-Yang, M. H. (2016). *Emotions, learning, and the brain: Exploring the educational implications of affective neuroscience.* New York: W. W. Norton.

Issa, F. A., Drummond, J., Cattaert, D., & Edwards, D. H. (2012). Neural circuit reconfiguration by social status. *Journal of Neuroscience, 32*(16), 5638–5645.

James, C., Weinstein, E., & Mendoza, K. (2019). *Teaching digital citizens in today's world: Research and insights behind the Common Sense K–12 Digital Citizenship Curriculum.* San Francisco: Common Sense Media. Retrieved from https://d1e2bohyu2u2w9.cloudfront.net/education/sites/default/files/tlr_component/common_sense_education_digital_citizenship_research_backgrounder.pdf

Jarvis, C. (2019). *30 days of genius with Chase Jarvis: Lesson 8: Brené Brown.* Retrieved from https://www.creativelive.com/class/30-days-genius-chase-jarvis/lessons/brene-brown

Joensson, M., Thomsen, K. R., Andersen, L. M., Gross, J., Mouridsen, K., Sandberg, K., et al. (2015). Making sense: Dopamine activates conscious self-monitoring through medial prefrontal cortex. *Human Brain Mapping, 36*(5), 1866–1877.

Johnson, D. W., Johnson, R. T., & Smith, K. A. (2013). Cooperative learning: Improving university instruction by basing practice on validated theory. *Journal on Excellence in College Teaching, 25*(3–4), 85–118.

Jones, S., Brush, K., Bailey, R., Brion-Meisels, G., McIntyre, J., Kahn, J., et al. (2017). *Navigating SEL from the inside out.* Harvard Graduate School of Education. Retrieved from https://www.wallacefoundation.org/knowledge-center/Documents/Navigating-Social-and-Emotional-Learning-from-the-Inside-Out.pdf

Kahneman, D. (2011). *Thinking, fast and slow.* New York: Farrar, Straus, & Giroux.

Kennon, J. (2019, November 8). Principal starts "no phone, new friends Friday" lunchtime tradition. ABC News KCRG.com. Retrieved from https://www.KCRG.com/content/news/Principal-starts-No-phone-new-friends-Friday-lunchtime-tradition--564682071.html

Kidd, C., Palmeri, H., & Aslin, R. N. (2013). Rational snacking: Young children's decision-making on the marshmallow task is moderated by beliefs about environmental reliability. *Cognition, 126*(1), 109–114.

Kidd, D., & Castano, E. (2013, October 18). Reading literary fiction improves theory of mind. *Science, 342*(6156), 377–380.

Knapp, M. L., & Hall, J. A. (2010). *Nonverbal communication in human interaction.* Boston: Cengage.

Korbey, H. (2017, October 27). The power of being seen. *Edutopia.* Retrieved from https://www.edutopia.org/article/power-being-seen

Landmark School Outreach. (n.d.). Responsible decision making (social emotional learning). Retrieved from https://www.landmarkoutreach. org/strategies/responsible-decision-making/

Lewis, M. (2012, October). Obama's way. *Vanity Fair.* Retrieved from https://www.vanityfair.com/news/2012/10/michael-lewis-profile-barack-obama

Lieberman, M. (2013). *Social: Why our brains are wired to connect.* New York: Crown Publishers.

Lieberman, M. (2019). The social brain and the workplace. *Talks at Google.* Retrieved from https://www.youtube.com/watch?v=h7UR9JwQEYk

Maslow, A. H. (1998). *Toward a psychology of being* (3rd ed.). Hoboken, NJ: Wiley.

Maynard, N., & Weinstein, B. (2019). *Hacking school discipline: 9 ways to create a culture of empathy and responsibility using restorative justice.* Highland Heights, OH: Times 10 Publications.

McTighe, J., & Willis, J. (2019). *Upgrade your teaching: Understanding by design meets neuroscience.* Alexandria, VA: ASCD.

Medina, J. (2014). *Brain rules for baby: How to raise a happy child from zero to five.* Seattle, WA: Pear Press.

Medina, J. (2017). *Brain rules for aging well: 10 principles for staying vital, happy, and sharp.* Seattle, WA: Pear Press.

Medina, J. (2018). *Attack of the teenage brain! Understanding and supporting the weird and wonderful adolescent learner.* Alexandria, VA: ASCD.

Merz, S. (2012, June 27). Teaching secrets: Get to know students through seating challenges. *Education Week.* Retrieved from https://www.edweek.org/tm/articles/2012/06/27/tln_merz.html

Mueller, P. A., & Oppenheimer, D. M. (2014). The pen is mightier than the keyboard: Advantages of longhand over laptop note taking. *Psychological Science, 25,* 1159–1168.

NameCoach. (2017, November 12). The brain on your name: How your brain responds to the sound of your name [Blog post]. Retrieved from https://name-coach.com/blog/brain-name-brain-responds-sound-name

National Child Traumatic Stress Network. (2019). *Secondary traumatic stress: Understanding the impact of trauma work on professionals* [Webinar]. Retrieved from https://www.nctsn.org/resources/secondary-traumatic-stress-understanding-the-impact-of-trauma-work-on-professionals

Padmanaban, D. (2017, April 12). Where empathy lives in the brain. *The Cut.* Retrieved from https://www.thecut.com/2017/04/where-empathy-lives-in-the-brain.html

Panksepp, J., & Biven, L. (2012). *The archaeology of mind: Neuroevolutionary origins of human emotions.* New York: Norton.

Pappas, S. (2012, February 1). The social mind: Brain region bigger in popular people. *Live Science*. Retrieved from https://www.livescience.com/18230-brain-area-friends.html

Parker, C. B. (2016, April 26). Teacher empathy reduces student suspensions, Stanford research shows. *Stanford News*. Retrieved from https://news.stanford.edu/2016/04/26/teacher-empathy-reduces-student-suspensions-stanford-research-shows/

Pearce, E., Wlodarski, R., Machin, A., & Dunbar, R. I. M. (2017). Variation in the ß-endorphin, oxytocin, and dopamine receptor genes is associated with different dimensions of human sociality. *PNAS, 114*(20), 5300–5305.

Perry, B. D. (2020). Understanding state-dependent functioning [Video]. *Neurosequential Network COVID-19 Stress, Distress, & Trauma Series: 2*. Retrieved from https://www.neurosequential.com/covid-19-resources

Perry, B. D., & Szalavitz, M. (2007). *The boy who was raised as a dog*. New York: Basic Books.

Plutchik, R. (1997). The circumplex as a general model of the structure of emotions and personality. In R. Plutchik & H. R. Conte (Eds.), *Circumplex models of personality and emotions* (pp. 17–45). Washington, DC: American Psychological Association.

Prothero, A. (2019, September 10). Can bite-sized lessons make social-emotional learning easier to teach? *Education Week*. Retrieved from https://www.edweek.org/ew/articles/2019/09/11/can-bite-sized-lessons-make-social-emotional-learning-easier.html

Quist, A., & Gregory, R. (2019). Teaching decision-making skills in the classroom. *The Arithmetic of Compassion*. Retrieved from https://www.arithmeticofcompassion.org/blog/2019/5/1/teaching-decision-making-skills-in-the-classroom

Reb, J., & Atkins, P. W. B. (Eds.). (2017). *Mindfulness in organizations: Foundations, research, and applications*. Cambridge, UK: Cambridge University Press.

Riess, H. (2018). *The empathy effect: Seven neuroscience-based keys for transforming the way we live, love, work, and connect across differences*. Boulder, CO: Sounds True.

Ripple Kindness Project. (2019, October 8). Crumpled paper–crumpled heart bullying exercise for all ages. Retrieved from https://ripplekindness.org/crumpled-paper-bullying-exercise/

Sanchez, H. (2015). *Designing a climate for closing the achievement gap* [Video]. Resiliency, Inc. Retrieved from https://www.youtube.com/watch?v=4E0sMLal8hk

Sapolsky, R. (2017). *Behave: The biology of humans at our best and worst*. New York: Penguin Books.

Schwartz, K. (2016). *I wish my teacher knew: How one question can change everything for our kids.* Boston: Da Capo Lifelong Books.

Shoda, Y., Mischel, W., & Peake, P. K. (1990). Predicting adolescent cognitive and self-regulatory competencies from preschool delay of gratification: Identifying diagnostic conditions. *Developmental Psychology, 26*(6), 978–986.

Siegel, D. (2014, August 12). How the teen brain transforms relationships. *Greater Good Magazine.* Retrieved from https://greatergood.berkeley.edu/article/item/how_the_teen_brain_transforms_relationships

Siegel, D. J., & Bryson, T. P. (2012). *The whole-brain child: 12 revolutionary strategies to nurture your child's developing mind.* New York: Bantam Books.

Siegel, D. J., & Bryson, T. (2018). *The yes brain: How to cultivate courage, curiosity, and resilience in your child.* New York: Bantam Books.

Silani, G., Lamm, C., Ruff, C., & Singer, T. (2013). Right supramarginal gyrus is crucial to overcome emotional egocentricity bias in social judgments. *The Journal of Neuroscience, 33*(39), 15466–15476.

Sinek, S. (2014). *Leaders eat last.* New York: Penguin Group.

Smith, D., Fisher, D. B., & Frey, N. E. (2015). *Better than carrots or sticks: Restorative practices for positive classroom management.* Alexandria, VA: ASCD.

Sokolov, A. A. (2018, June 5). The cerebellum in social cognition. *Frontiers in Cellular Neuroscience.* Retrieved from doi:10.3389/fncel.2018.00145

Souers, K., & Hall, P. (2016). *Fostering resilient learners: Strategies for creating a trauma-sensitive classroom.* Alexandria, VA: ASCD.

Sousa, D. (2015). *How the brain influences behavior.* New York: Skyhorse Publishing.

Sprenger, M. (2018). *How to teach so students remember* (2nd ed.). Alexandria, VA: ASCD.

Srinivasan, M. (2019, April 10). Promoting social and emotional learning at home. *Education.com Blog.* Retrieved from https://www.education.com/blog/whats-new/selathome/

Srinivasan, R., Golomb, J. D., & Martinez, A. (2016). A neural basis of facial action recognition in humans. *Journal of Neuroscience, 36*(16), 4434–4442.

Stiggins, R. (2017). *The perfect assessment system.* Alexandria, VA: ASCD.

Stosny, S. (2013, September 6). The good and the bad of journaling [Blog post]. *Psychology Today.* Retrieved from https://www.psychologytoday.com/us/blog/anger-in-the-age-entitlement/201309/the-good-and-the-bad-journaling

Sylwester, R. (1995). *A celebration of neurons: An educator's guide to the human brain.* Alexandria, VA: ASCD.

Szalavitz, M., & Perry, B. D. (2010). *Born for love: Why empathy is essential— And endangered*. New York: HarperCollins.

Tantillo Philibert, C. (2016). *Everyday SEL in elementary school: Integrating social-emotional learning and mindfulness into your classroom*. New York: Routledge.

Tate, E. (2019, November 15). Rethinking recess leads to results on and off the playground. *EdSurge*. Retrieved from https://www.edsurge.com/news/2019-11-15-rethinking-recess-leads-to-results-on-and-off-the-playground

Teaching Tolerance Staff. (2019, May 6). What is "mix it up at lunch"? Retrieved from https://www.tolerance.org/magazine/what-is-mix-it-up-at-lunch

Toth, M. D., & Sousa, D. A. (2019). *The power of student teams: Achieving social, emotional, and cognitive learning in every classroom through academic teaming*. West Palm Beach, FL: Learning Sciences International.

Uhls, Y. T., Michikyan, M., Morris, J., Garcia, D., Small, G. W., Zgourou, E., et al. (2014, October). Five days at outdoor education camp without screens improves preteen skills with nonverbal emotion cues. *Computers in Human Behavior, 39*, 387–392.

van der Kolk, B. (2014). *The body keeps the score: Brain, mind, and body in the healing of trauma*. New York: Viking Penguin.

WeAreTeachers Staff. (2018, March 6). 10 tips for teaching emotional regulation (& improving classroom behavior at the same time). Retrieved from https://www.weareteachers.com/emotional-regulation/

Willis, J. (2012). How to build happy middle school brains. *MiddleWeb*. Retrieved from https://www.middleweb.com/2847/how-to-build-happy-brains/

Wlodkowski, R. J. (1983). *Motivational opportunities for successful teaching* [Leader's guide]. Phoenix, AZ: Universal Dimensions.

Wolfe, P. (2010). *Brain matters: Translating research into classroom practice* (2nd ed.). Alexandria, VA: ASCD.

Wong, H., & Wong, R. (2013, October). How to start class every day. *Teachers.Net Gazette*. Retrieved from https://www.teachers.net/wong/OCT13/

Wong, H. K., & Wong, R. T. (2018). *The first days of school: How to be an effective teacher* (5th ed.). Mountain View, CA: Harry K. Wong Publications.

Zak, P. J. (2013, December 17). How stories change the brain. *Greater Good Magazine*. Retrieved from https://greatergood.berkeley.edu/article/item/how_stories_change_brain

Zalanick, M. (2019, April 8). Best (practices) in show: Therapy dogs in schools. *District Administration*. Retrieved from https://districtadministration.com/best-practices-show-therapy-dogs-in-schools/

Index

Note: Page references followed by an italicized *f* indicate information contained in figures.

compassionate empathy, 43
compassion fatigue, 186–187
constructive controversy activity,
   175
control, 95
conversations, face-to-face, 51
conver-stations activity, 176–177
cooperative learning, 140, 146–147
coregulation, 86
cortisol, 5, 17, 23, 66, 87, 183–184
cotton ball breathing, 102
Covey, Stephen, 36, 42
crumpled hearts strategy, 55–56
curiosity, 7

Dear Abby activity, 176
debating, 173–175
decision fatigue, 187–188
decision making. *See* responsible
   decision making
The Deepest Well (Burke Harris), 92
delayed gratification, 89, 110
discussion tasks, 133
disgust, 68*f*
dogs, therapy, 100–101
dopamine, 5, 7, 18, 23, 66–67, 87,
   139–140, 163
drawing, 76–77
Dweck, Carol, 82
dysregulation, 86, 92

egocentrism, 43–45. *See also*
   empathy
emotional coaching, 63
emotional empathy, 43
Emotional Intelligence (Goleman), 3
emotion planners, 104–105, 105*f*
emotions
   alexithymia, 79
   brain function of, 65–66, 65*f*
   and brain processing, 5
   and decision making, 188–190

emotions—(*continued*)
   self-awareness and, 63, 64
   social awareness and, 121–122
   suppressing, 79–80
emotion vocabulary, 67–69, 68*f,* 114
empathic concern, 43
empathy
   about, 8, 39–40
   appreciation notes, 49–50
   "ask, don't tell" approach, 49
   brain function and, 41–42,
      43–46, 44*f*
   classroom pets, 52–53
   cognitive empathy, 42
   community service projects, 52
   compassionate empathy, 43
   crumpled hearts strategy, 55–56
   developing, 40–42
   development strategies, 46–59
   emotional empathy, 43
   "Epiphany in a Paper Bag" strat-
      egy, 54–55
   face-to-face conversations, 51
   if/then statements, 59–60
   importance of, 1
   kindness walls, 50
   literature and, 53–54
   lunch table seating, 53
   modeling, 40–41, 47–49
   and social awareness, 114,
      122–124
   teacher self-assessment of,
      57–59
   types of, 42–43
   and understanding, 42, 49
   volunteer work, 52
endorphins, 5, 139
"Epiphany in a Paper Bag" strategy,
   54–55
equity stick, 28
establish-maintain-restore (EMR)
   method, 35–36

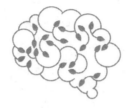

About the Author

Marilee Sprenger is an international educational consultant in the fields of social-emotional learning, literacy, vocabulary, and brain research. She was a classroom teacher for 25 years, mainly at the middle school level. In 1992, she trained and traveled with author and brain-based-learning educator Eric Jensen and discovered her love for the brain. She has authored 13 books related to the brain, learning, and memory; written numerous articles; and developed DVDs, webinars, quick reference guides, and online courses available through ASCD. Her keynote and workshop competence makes her a sought-after speaker for schools, districts, educational service centers, regional offices of education, and educational conferences. Sprenger is a member of the American Academy of Neurology. You can reach her through her website, marileesprenger.com, e-mail brainlady@gmail.com, or on Twitter @MarileeSprenger.

Related ASCD Resources

At the time of publication, the following resources were available (ASCD stock numbers appear in parentheses).

Print Products

All Learning Is Social and Emotional: Helping Students Develop Essential Skills for the Classroom and Beyond by Nancy Frey, Douglas Fisher, and Dominique Smith (#119033)

Attack of the Teenage Brain! Understanding and Supporting the Weird and Wonderful Adolescent Learner by John Medina (#118024)

Creating a Trauma-Sensitive Classroom (Quick Reference Guide) by Kristin Souers and Pete Hall (#QRG118054)

Developing Growth Mindsets: Principles and Practices for Maximizing Students' Potential by Donna Wilson and Marcus Conyers (#120033)

Engage the Brain: How to Design for Learning That Taps into the Power of Emotion by Allison Posey (#119015)

How to Teach So Students Remember, 2nd Edition by Marilee Sprenger (#118016)

Learning That Sticks: A Brain-Based Model for Instructional Design and Delivery by Bryan Goodwin, Tonia Gibson, and Kristin Rouleau (#120032)

Mindfulness in the Classroom: Strategies for Promoting Concentration, Compassion, and Calm by Thomas Armstrong (#120018)

Relationship, Responsibility, and Regulation: Trauma-Invested Practices for Fostering Resilient Learners by Kristin Van Marter Souers with Pete Hall (#119027)

Research-Based Strategies to Ignite Student Learning: Insights from Neuroscience and the Classroom, Revised and Expanded Edition by Judy Willis and Malana Willis (#120029)

Taking Social-Emotional Learning Schoolwide: The Formative Five Success Skills for Students and Staff by Thomas R. Hoerr (#120014)

Teaching to Strengths: Supporting Students Living with Trauma, Violence, and Chronic Stress by Debbie Zacarian, Lourdes Alvarez-Ortiz, and Judie Haynes (#117035)

For up-to-date information about ASCD resources, go to **www.ascd.org.** You can search the complete archives of *Educational Leadership* at **www.ascd.org/el.**

DVDs

All Learning Is Social and Emotional: The Hidden Curriculum by Nancy E. Frey, Douglas B. Fisher, and Dominique Smith (#620046VS)

Teaching the Adolescent Brain DVD with Facilitator's Guide (#606050)

PD Online

The Brain: Developing Lifelong Learning Habits, 2nd Edition (#PD11OC136S)

Fostering Resilient Learners by Kristin Souers and Peter Hall (#PD11OC001S)

ASCD myTeachSource®

Download resources from a professional learning platform with hundreds of research-based best practices and tools for your classroom at http://myteachsource.ascd.org/.

For more information, send an e-mail to member@ascd.org; call 1-800-933-2723 or 703-578-9600; send a fax to 703-575-5400; or write to Information Services, ASCD, 1703 N. Beauregard St., Alexandria, VA 22311-1714 USA.

The ASCD Whole Child approach is an effort to transition from a focus on narrowly defined academic achievement to one that promotes the long-term development and success of all children. Through this approach, ASCD supports educators, families, community members, and policymakers as they move from a vision about educating the whole child to sustainable, collaborative actions.

Social-Emotional Learning and the Brain relates to the **healthy, safe, engaged,** and **supported** tenets. *For more about the ASCD Whole Child approach, visit* **www.ascd.org/ wholechild.**

WHOLE CHILD
TENETS

1 **HEALTHY**
Each student enters school healthy and learns about and practices a healthy lifestyle.

2 **SAFE**
Each student learns in an environment that is physically and emotionally safe for students and adults.

3 **ENGAGED**
Each student is actively engaged in learning and is connected to the school and broader community.

4 **SUPPORTED**
Each student has access to personalized learning and is supported by qualified, caring adults.

5 **CHALLENGED**
Each student is challenged academically and prepared for success in college or further study and for employment and participation in a global environment.